Contents

10650937

Preface

This little book aims to introduce the Thai language. It is intended for those who know nothing about it, but are keen to learn. We use the method of selecting 100 key words, and using these to make up sentences and present a range of expressions, so that you can "say 1000 things."

The words are arranged as ten topics, ones that will be helpful for the various situations you might find yourself in when visiting Thailand, traveling about and meeting Thai people. The language used is authentic, and contains many clues about Thai culture and society. There are also grammatical and cultural notes to help clarify things. An English-Thai wordlist gives the same vocabulary, but in reverse order, so that you can refer to it like a mini dictionary.

To help with the pronunciation we give the Thai in a simple system of romanization. Many systems exist. Ours is not meant to be scientific, merely useful for speakers of English. Thai script has also been inserted, so that Thai friends can help you to get the sounds right, and of course later on you might want to learn to read it yourself.

The Thai language is very different from English. But it is the key to learning about the people and culture of this fascinating country. So we would like to encourage you to have a go, use some Thai, and have the satisfaction of communicating successfully in this wonderful language.

Chohk dii! โชคดี Good luck!
Stuart Robson and Prateep Changchit

Revised Edition

Instant,
THAI

How to Express Over 1,000 Different Ideas
With Just 100 Key Words and Phrases!

by Stuart Robson & Prateep Changchit
revised by Jintana Rattanakhemakorn

TUTTLE Publishing

Tokyo | Rutland, Vermont | Singapore

About the Thai language

Thai is the official language of the Kingdom of Thailand, and as such it is used by about sixty-five million people. It is taught and spoken over the whole country. Standard Thai is based on the language of the capital, Bangkok, as used by educated people.

Not surprisingly, there are several varieties of Thai, to be found in various parts of the country, namely:

- Central Thai, found in the central plain, and including Bangkok

- North-eastern Thai, also called Lao as it borders on Laos; many speakers of this variety come to Bangkok to work

- Northern Thai, centred on the ancient city of Chiang Mai; and

- Southern Thai, found in peninsular Thailand, where the main centre is Nakhon Si Thammarat.

The differences between these varieties are significant, involving different tones and different vocabulary, but are not enough to warrant calling them separate languages. Sharing regional forms of the language brings a sense of identity, and most people are proud to use them when they meet others from the same area. The regional varieties of Thai are not normally written (only spoken); to write them would involve changing the tones and hence the spelling. The standard written language reflects the pronunciation and style of central

Thailand and the capital, the center of government. As well as regional variants, there are of course also differences in speech depending on a person's social class or educational level.

As well as Thai in its several forms, we must not forget that there are other languages spoken within the borders of the country, such as:

- Malay, an important Austronesian language, found in the four southernmost provinces, bordering on Malaysia

- Karen, a Sino-Tibetan language, spoken by several groups in the mountains along the Burmese border

- Lisu, Akha, Lahu, Hmong and Yao, also Sino-Tibetan languages spoken in the mountainous parts of the north; and

- Khmer (or Cambodian), an Austroasiatic language, spoken in an area bordering on northern Cambodia.

This raises the question of ethnicity. Communities speaking these non-Thai languages are of course Thai in the sense of being subjects of the King, although they may not participate to the same extent in mainstream Thai culture, and may prefer to keep their own linguistic and cultural identity. Foreign visitors often enjoy traveling to see these "hill tribes" and their culture.

Thai belongs to a language-family called Tai. This includes Thai and its neighbor and close relative Lao, as well as Tai Yai or Shan, spoken in parts of northern Mynmar, Zhuang, a major language of southern China, Nung or Black and White Tai spoken by ethnic minorities in northern Vietnam, and the extinct Ahom found as far west as Assam in north-east India.

Thai entered the present Thailand only comparatively recently (11th and 12th centuries) from the north, and in this process came into contact with the Khmer and Mon who were already living there. As a result of this contact, we find many Khmer loanwords in present-day Thai. Some examples are:

tamruat	ตำรวจ	policeman
gamlang	กำลัง	strength
dtalaat	ตลาด	market
taleh	ทะเล	sea

There are also a large number of loanwords based on Pali (the sacred language of Theravada Buddhism) and Sanskrit (the ancient language of India), coined for the purpose of creating the terms needed for modern life, e.g.

thohrasap	telephone
sukhaphaap	health
wattanatham	culture

And there are many more taken directly from English, e.g.

thiiwii	TV
sehrok	photocopy (xerox!)
chek bin	may I pay the bill?
hoten	hotel
bai-bai	bye-bye!

Basic Thai is monosyllabic, and loanwords all seem to have two or more syllables. You can see that certain sounds have been changed in the process of adoption into the Thai language.

Thai is a tonal language. In other words, the pitch on which a word is pronounced can be important, as it may distinguish it from another, similar, word with a different pitch. There are five tones. Tones are inherent, that is to say, they are a "built-in" element of the word. When you learn Thai you have to learn the tone of each word—this is not something you can put off till a later date (on tones, see pages 14–15). In fact, there are rules related to the form and spelling of words that help you to predict what their tone will be. By the way, Thai is not related to Chinese or Vietnamese, which also happen to be tonal.

Thai has its own script (or writing system), that was developed in the 13th century to write its particular sounds, and is based on Khmer script. This system is basically syllabic (not actually an alphabet), and is related not only to Khmer and Cham script, but also Burmese, Javanese and Balinese scripts, all of which derive ultimately from a script used in South India in the early common era (A.D.), and which was brought into Southeast Asia with the spread of Indian civilization, which included Buddhism and Hinduism and their scriptures.

It is possible to represent the sounds of Thai in the familiar Western script (called roman), although there are a few problems with this, and various methods have been used. We have attempted to devise a system that is not only accurate but also not too difficult for the beginning student to understand and read (please see 9–15). We also include the Thai script for each item in this book, so that Thai friends can help you with pronunciation (Thais are generally not familiar with a romanization of their language).

Note that Thai has its own "alphabetical" order, which you will need to learn if you want to master Thai script and use a Thai-English dictionary.

Spelling and Pronunciation

This section aims to show the spelling system that we have adopted for this book and, where necessary, to explain how to pronounce the letters and combinations of letters. This system is in fact not a transliteration, in the sense that one Thai sign is always represented by one roman letter, and it thus does not attempt to reproduce the spelling of Thai (as found in the Thai script). It is hoped that the method used will be clear and helpful for English-speaking readers.

To facilitate the discussion, we look first at the consonants, and then at the vowel sounds, giving an example word and the Thai spelling. The pronunciation is as in English, except where indicated otherwise.

Consonants

This is the same sound as the *ng* in "si<u>ng</u>"; when it comes at the beginning of a word, it may be hard to say. Try saying "si<u>ng</u>er," then slowing it down and breaking it into two parts: "si-nger." Then you can get *ng* in an initial position.

g	**gài**	ไก่	chicken (as in "<u>g</u>et")
kh	**khài**	ไข่	egg (as in "<u>k</u>it")
ng	**nguu**	งู	snake (as in "si<u>ng</u>" or "si<u>ng</u>er")
j	**jaan**	จาน	plate (as in "<u>j</u>am")
ch	**chórn**	ช้อน	spoon (as in "<u>ch</u>at")
s	**sìi**	สี่	four (as in "<u>s</u>it")

d	***dèk***	เด็ก	child (as in "do")
dt	***dtaa***	ตา	eye (as in "stone")

NOTE: This is like a *t* but with no wind behind it. You can get this effect by pursing the lips before releasing the sound.

th	***Thai***	ไทย	Thai (as in "teach")
n	***norn***	นอน	to lie down (as in "nine")
b	***bâan***	บ้าน	house (as in "bed")
bp	***bplaa***	ปลา	fish (as in "spy")
ph	***phâa***	ผ้า	cloth (as in "pan")

This sound is an ordinary *p*, but with wind behind it. It is never *ph* as in "photo" (we have another letter for the *f* sound).

f	***fan***	ฟัน	tooth (as in "fine")
m	***maew***	แมว	cat (as in "make")
y	***yaa***	ยา	medicine (as in "you")
r	***rórn***	ร้อน	hot, temperature (as in "rat")
l	***lom***	ลม	wind (as in "lot")
w	***wát***	วัด	temple (as in "well")
h	***hông***	ห้อง	room (as in "hand")

plus a glottal stop that is not normally written (but has a role in pronunciation) and will be represented with an apostrophe when needed, for example, *jà'*.

Vowels

Apart from the differences between tones (to be discussed on page 18), there is also an essential difference between long and short vowels. To mark this, we simply write the vowel sound double—that is, it has to be sounded as longer than the short one.

a   ***wan***   วัน   day
The example sounds like English "won." The *a* is like the *a* in "h<u>a</u>!" It is never the a of English "c<u>a</u>t" (this exists as well, though—see page 16).

aa   ***maa***   มา   to come
This could be written *ah*; the example word sounds like English "mar," but of course without any *r* attached to it.

i   ***prík***   พริก   chilli
This is a short sound, as in English "<u>if</u>."

ii   ***mii***   มี   to have
This is the long version of the above; think of the *ee* in "s<u>ee</u>."

u   ***khun***   คุณ   you (polite)
This is the short sound as found in English "f<u>oo</u>t" or "p<u>u</u>t."

uu   ***nguu***   งู   snake
This is the long version of the above, like the *oo* in English "m<u>oo</u>d."

The next group of sounds is a little more difficult:

oh   ***giloh***   กิโล   kilo
This is the *o* of English "g<u>o</u>," to be carefully distinguished from the next two sounds.

o   ***lom***   ลม   wind
As in English "fr<u>o</u>m."

or   ***lor***   หล่อ   handsome
The sound intended here is the English *or*, but without any "r" attached to it; it could also be represented with *aw*, as in "<u>aw</u>ful."

eu   ***meu***   มือ   hand
There are short and long versions of this sound. It is like the *eu* of French "deux," but tighter. Compare *oe* below.

ae   ***láe***   และ   and
This is the *a* sound of "cat." Note the glottal stop on the end, making the sound short.

e   ***lék***   เล็ก   small
This is just the *e* of English "met."

eh   ***mehk***   เมฆ   cloud
This is like the *e* acute of French, rather than English *ay*; it could also be written with *air* (no "r" sound attached), but is a pure vowel, not a diphthong.

oe   ***thoe***   เธอ   you (familiar pronoun)
Like the *ir* of "bird" (no "r" attached); or the *ö* of German.
There are long and short versions.

Next, there is a wonderful array of diphthongs, that is, combinations of two (or more) vowels. The sounds are as indicated above, but run together, as follows:

ia	***mia*** [pronounce like *mee-ah*]	เมีย	wife (informal)
iu	***hǐu*** [*hew*]	หิว	hungry
eua	***reua*** [*rer-ah*]	เรือ	boat
ua	***wua*** [*woo-ah*]	วัว	cow
ai	***yài*** [rhymes with *hi!*]	ใหญ่	big
ao	***mau*** [*mow*, rhymes with *wow!*]	เมา	drunk
ui	***khui*** [*kooy*]	คุย	to chat
oi	***noi*** [*noy*]	น้อย	a little
oei	***khoei*** [*ker-y*]	เคย	ever

euai	**nèuai** [ner-ay]	เหนื่อย	tired
io	**dio** [dee-oh]	เดียว	alone
eho	**leho** [lay-oh]	เลว	bad
aeo	**maeo** [mair-oh]	แมว	cat
iau	**nĭau** [nee-ow]	เหนียว	sticky

Tones

This is an especially interesting feature of the Thai language, one that gives it a pleasant "singing" sound. The tones are essential, as mentioned above, and not an optional extra. Every Thai word can be said to have a tone, that is, has to be pronounced on a particular pitch. Changing the tone may, in some cases, produce a different word—sometimes with amusing or embarrassing results.

There are five tones in Thai. We call them:

- mid
- high
- falling
- low, and
- rising.

We have marks to indicate these. Each one has its typical contour.

The majority of words are **mid tone**, so no mark is used for them. When pronouncing a **mid tone**, we have to be careful to hold the note steadily, not let it drop or rise.

The **high tone** starts higher than mid, and rises to a little "hook" at the end.

The **falling tone** starts high, and then drops.

The **low tone** sounds like an English emphatic tone: "No!"

The **rising tone** starts low and then goes up.

Native speakers of Thai have very sharp ears for these differences, and so in natural speech the distinctions are sometimes minimal, and may be slurred over when words are in combination. But the learner is well advised to produce the tones exactly, and even to exaggerate them, in order to hit the right note. You can practice by "conducting" with your hand in the air.

In some of the example words already given, some tone marks can already be seen; a complete set looks like this:

Bpaa	ปา	throw	(mid tone)	¯
Bpàa	ป่า	forest	(low tone)	`
Bpâa	ป้า	aunt	(falling tone)	^
Bpáa	ป๊า	father (Chinese)	(high tone)	´
Bpǎa	ป๋า	father (Papa)	(rising tone)	ˇ

Please note that when a vowel sound is written with two letters, the mark is placed over the first, but this of course applies to both.

Getting to know you

People traveling in Thailand will obviously want to become better informed about everything they see about them and will seek social contact with Thais. The best way to make contact is to exchange a few words in Thai. Your Thai friends will be pleased, and will help you with the pronunciation.

1 DII ดี Good! Right! Okay!

Sawatdii. สวัสดี **Hello!**

This is an all-purpose word of greeting. It can be used with anybody, and at any time of day. Informally, people just say *Wàtdii!* หวัดดี. You can use it to say "hello" on the phone, and also to say goodbye. (It isn't actually derived from *dii* ดี at all, but is useful to include here.)

Sabai dii mái? สบายดีไหม **Are you well?**

To answer a question like this, just repeat the main word (without the question word):

Sabai dii. สบายดี **Yes, I am.**

Dii mái? ดีไหม **Is that okay? Do you agree?**

Chohk dii. โชคดี **Good luck.**

Yin dii. ยินดี **It's my pleasure.**

Dii jai. ดีใจ **Happy** (to see you, know you; literally "good in my heart").

Grammatical notes

1. Thai sentence is simply formed by 'subject-verb-object' order like English. No word is modified or conjugated for tense, person, possession, singular or plural, gender, or subject-verb agreement.

2. The question word *mái* ไหม is placed at the end of a sentence. It can be interpreted as both a general question and an invitation or suggestion. To answer "yes" repeat the verb or adjective. For saying "no", put *mâi* ไม่ before the verb or adjective.

   Question: subject + verb/adjective + *mái*
   Yes: subject + verb/adjective
   No: subject + *mâi* (no) + verb/adjective

3. In Thai sentence, subject omission is acceptable when it is clear who the subject is.

Cultural note

Thais do not shake hands, nor do they say "please to meet you" when they "meet and greet" someone. Thais use a gesture of *wâai* ไหว้. They make a slight bow with the palms pressed together, as a way of greeting and respecting one another. There is a certain "protocol" for making the *wâai* ไหว้, bearing in mind its function, namely to express respect. So we *wâai* ไหว้ "up," to someone we want to show respect to, including a new acquaintance. If someone makes a *wâai* ไหว้ to you, you must return it (if you're carrying something, then one hand will do, or even just a little bow). Consequently, you do not make a *wâai* ไหว้ to a younger or junior person first (but you do return it), and of course you never make one to a child.

When it is intended as a form of greeting or farewell, people would say *sà-wàt-dii* สวัสดี while performing the *wâi*.

2 KHÁ/KHÂ/KHRÁP คะ/ค่ะ/ครับ
Polite particles

These three words should be introduced at an early stage, because they are very common. They are used to end a sentence in order to make an utterance sound very polite and respectful.

- ค่ะ *khâ* (for women) is used for making statements, commands, and also used alone as a polite way to answer "yes".

- คะ *khá* (for women) is used at the end of a question.

- ครับ *khráp* is a neutral ending for men to use in any situation.

3 CHÊU ชื่อ name

Khun chêu à-rai. คุณชื่ออะไร
What is your name?

Phŏm chêu Simon. ผมชื่อไซมอน
My name is Simon.

Chăn chêu Helen. ฉันชื่อเฮเลน
My name is Helen.

Khău chêu Richard. เขาชื่อ ริดชาร์ด
His name is Richard.

Khun mii chêu lên mái? คุณมีชื่อเล่นไหม
Do you have a nickname?

Grammatical notes

1. The word *chêu* ชื่อ can be translated into the English word "name" or with the verb "to be called."

2. Thai has a complicated set of personal pronouns.

The following are appropriate pronouns for conversational use.

I/me	*chăn*	ฉัน (female)
	dì-chăn	ดิฉัน (formal for female)
	phŏm	ผม (male)

We	*rao*	เรา
You	*khun*	คุณ
	thoe	เธอ (female)
He/She/They	*khǎo*	เขา
	thoe	เธอ (she)

Cultural notes

Thais call each other by given names. However, nick-names are commonly used in Thailand. Thais may give you their nicknames instead of their first names. In general Thai given names are preceded by Khun (Mr., Mrs., or Miss), unless they carry a title, such as doctor. Khun is used for men and women, married or single. For example: Somjai (given name) + Rattana (family name) is Khun Somjai. If you don't know a person's name, address them as Khun. The first name and the family name are introduced in an official introduction,

4 RÚU-JÀK รู้จัก to know, be acquainted

Khun rúu-jàk Mali mái? คุณ รู้จักมะลิ ไหม
Do you know Mali?

Thoe rúu-jàk rong-raem Oriental mái?
เธอรู้จักโรงแรมโอเรียนเต็ลไหม
Do you know the Oriental Hotel?

→ *Mâi rúu-jàk.* ไม่รู้จัก **No, I don't.**

Grammatical notes

Mâi ไม่ ("no, not") is used for a negative sentence and is always placed in front of verbs or adjectives.

Mâi sabai. ไม่สบาย **(I'm) not feeling well.**

Mâi dii. ไม่ดี **(That's) not good (not a good thing, not a good idea).**

Mâi au. ไม่เอา **I don't want it (I won't accept it,** literally "not take").

Mâi chôrp. ไม่ชอบ **(I) don't like it.**

Mâi sŏnjai. ไม่สนใจ **(I'm) not interested.**

Mâi sŭay. ไม่สวย
(It's) not beautiful. (I don't find it attractive.)

Mâi bpen rai. ไม่เป็นไร **No worries! It's okay! It doesn't matter! Not at all!**

NOTE: Many people say *mâi-pen-rai* because they believe that they don't have much control over things. Just accept and move on.

5   YÙU   อยู่   to be there, present; to live, dwell

Khun Wichaa yùu mái? คุณวิชาอยู่ไหม
Is Mr Wichaa there? (= Is Mr Wichaa in?)

Tim yùu thîi nǎi? ทิมอยู่ที่ไหน
Where is Tim?

Tim yùu thîi bâan. ทิมอยู่ที่บ้าน
Tim is at home.

Bâan gèut yùu thîi nǎi? บ้านเกิดอยู่ที่ไหน
Where is your home town ("village of birth")?

Chǎn yùu thîi Melbourne. ฉันอยู่ที่เมลเบอร์น
I live in Melbourne.

For a different meaning of *yùu* อยู่, see Note at the end
of Word 7 below.

6   KHON   คน   person, people

Khun bpen khon châat à-rai? คุณเป็นคนชาติอะไร
What is your nationality?

→ *Khǎu bpen khon Amerigan.* เขาเป็นคนอเมริกัน
   He's an American.

NOTE: the place is *Amerigaa* อเมริกา; and the adjective
is *Amerigan*.

Khǎu bpen khon Jiin. เขาเป็นคนจีน **He's Chinese.**

Yîi-bpùn ญี่ปุ่น **Japanese**

Yeraman เยอรมัน **German**

Faràngsèt ฝรั่งเศส **French**

Anggrìt อังกฤษ **British**

("English" covers the whole of Britain!)

NOTE: The same adjectives for nationality generally apply to the language, e.g.:

Phaasǎa Jiin ภาษาจีน **Chinese (language)**

Yîi-bpùn ญี่ปุ่น **Japanese**

Faràngsèt ฝรั่งเศส **French**

Thai ไทย **Thai**

Anggrìt อังกฤษ **English**

---

7   THAM ทำ **to do; to make**

Khun tham à-rai? คุณทำอะไร
What do you do? or **What are you doing?**

→ *Chǎn tham ahǎan.* ฉันทำอาหาร
   I'm cooking (literally **"making food"**).

→ *Phǒm duu tiiwii yùu.* ผมดูทีวีอยู่
   I'm watching TV.

→ *Chăn norn lên yùu.* ฉันนอนเล่นอยู่
I'm taking a nap.

→ *Chăn shopping yùu.* ฉันชอบปิ้งอยู่
I'm shopping.

NOTE: In order to show continuous or present action, it is usually expressed by adding *yùu* อยู่ at the end of the sentence.

Khun tham-ngaan à-rai? คุณทำงานอะไร
What do you do for living?
(literally "What is your job?")

→ *Phŏm pen nák-thú-rá-kìt.* ผมเป็นนักธุรกิจ
I'm a businessman.

→ *Chăn pen phá-yaa-baan.* ฉันเป็นพยาบาล
I'm a nurse.

nák-rórng นักร้อง **a singer**

nák-gilaa นักกีฬา **sportsman/woman, athlete**

nák-dtên นักเต้น **dancer**

nák-muay นักมวย **boxer**

nák-sùek-săa นักศึกษา **university student**

aa-jaan อาจารย์ **professor/lecturer**

măw หมอ **doctor**

thá-naay-khwaam ทนายความ **lawyer**

tam-rùat ตำรวจ **police officer**

phá-nák-ngaan พนักงาน **office worker**

phá-nák-ngaan khǎay พนักงานขาย **salesperson**

thá-hǎan ทหาร **soldier**

khâa-râat-chá-kaan ข้าราชการ **government official**

wít-sà-wá-gawn วิศวกร **engineer**

châang ช่าง **mechanic**

Grammatical note

Verb-to-be *pen* (เป็น) is used with a noun to indicate attributes, properties, or identity of a subject. For example:

Phǒm pen mǎw. ผมเป็นหมอ **I am a doctor.**

Chǎn pen khon Thai. ฉันเป็นคนไทย **I am Thai.**

8 DTORN ตอน **part of the day**

dtorn cháau ตอนเช้า **in the morning**

dtorn thîang ตอนเที่ยง **at noon**

dtorn bàai ตอนบ่าย **in the afternoon**

dtorn yen ตอนเย็น **in the evening**

dtorn khâm ตอนค่ำ **iate at night**

Dtorn cháau rau bpai <u>hông-náam</u>.

ตอนเช้าเราไปห้องน้ำ

In the morning we go to <u>the bathroom</u> (toilet).

Substitute the word underlined:

gin aahăan cháau กินอาหารเช้า **have breakfast**

àap náam อาบน้ำ **take a bath**

bpraeng fan แปรงฟัน **clean our teeth**

wĭi phŏm หวีผม **brush our hair**

dtàeng dtua แต่งตัว **get dressed**

hăa wâen-dtaa หาแว่นตา **go looking for our glasses**

Dtorn thîang rau bpai gin ahǫan-thîang.

ตอนเที่ยงเราไปกินอาหารเที่ยง

At noon we have lunch.

Dtorn bàai rau bpai gin ahǫan-wâang.

ตอนบ่ายเราไปกินอาหารว่าง

In the afternoon we have a snack.

Dtorn yen rau bpai gin ahǫan yen.

ตอนเย็นเราไปกินอาหารเย็น

In the evening we eat dinner.

Dtorn khâm rau bpai disago.

ตอนค่ำเราไปดิสโก้

In the dead of night we go to a disco.

9   LÁEW แล้ว   already; past tense marker

Sèt láew. เสร็จแล้ว
It's finished (has been done).

Mòt láew. หมดแล้ว
It's all used up (finished).

Jàai láew. จ่ายแล้ว
(I've) paid already.

Khâu-jai láew. เข้าใจแล้ว
I understand (literally "understand already").

Fŏn dtòk láew. ฝนตกแล้ว
It's raining (has started to rain).

Grammatical note

This is a very important word. It is the only way we
can express a past tense in Thai. But we don't always
need to translate it with a past tense, as the examples
show, if it is already clear that the process is complete
or the condition has been achieved. It always comes in
a final position. See also the next word.

YANG ยัง **not yet; still**

Gin yaa rúe yang? กินยาหรือยัง
Have you taken the medicine yet?
(literally "not yet").

→ *Gin láew.* กินแล้ว **I have ... .**

Phóp Khun Fernando rúe yang?
พบคุณเฟอร์นานโดหรือยัง
Have you met Fernando yet?

→ *Yang.* ยัง **Not yet.**

→ *Khǎu yang yùu thîi Chumporn.*
เขายังอยู่ที่ชุมพร
He's still in Chumporn.

Grammatical note

Rúe yang หรือยัง is used to ask whether someone has done something previously or has done something yet. It's always placed at the end of a sentence.

- To say "yes" put *láew* แล้ว (already) after the verb.
- To answer "no" just say *yang* ยัง (not yet) in short or put *yang mâi* ยังไม่..... (not....yet) before the verb.

Asking questions and getting answers

11 **À-RAI** อะไร **what?**

Nîi à-rai? นี่อะไร **What is this (close by)?**

→ *Nîi nangsĕu.* นี่หนังสือ **This is a book.**

Nân à-rai? นั่นอะไร
What is that (further away)?

→ *Nân wát.* นั่นวัด **That's a temple.**

An nîi à-rai? อันนี้อะไร
What is this (item)?

→ *An nîi nangsĕu-deun-thaang.*
อันนี้หนังสือเดินทาง
This is a passport.

An nán à-rai? อันนั้นอะไร
What is that (item)?

→ *An nán gra-bpǎu.* อันนั้นกระเป๋า
  That is a bag (piece of baggage).

Grammatical note

You may have detected the difference in tone between
nîi นี่ and *níi* นี้. This is because they have a different
function, even though both have been translated with
"this." When it stands by itself as a sort of pronoun ("this
something") then it is pronounced *nîi* นี่, but when it
describes (and follows) a noun, then it is pronounced *níi*
นี้. This means that in the above examples the word *an*
อัน is a noun. In fact it is a useful little word, "thing."

11 THÎI NǍI ที่ไหน where?

Khun yùu thîi nǎi? คุณอยู่ที่ไหน
Where do you live?

→ *Phǒm yùu thîi Grungthêhp.* ผมอยู่ที่กรุงเทพ
  [usually spelled Krungthep] **I live in Bangkok.**

Bâan (khǒrng) khun yùu thîi nǎi?
บ้าน (ของ) คุณอยู่ที่ไหน
Where is your house/home?

→ *Thîi thanŏn Sukhumwit.* ที่ถนนสุขุมวิท
   In Sukhumwit Road.

Khun jà' bpai thîi năi? คุณจะไปที่ไหน
Where are you going (where will you go)?

→ *Phŏm jà' bpai thîi rong-raem.*
   ผมจะไปที่โรงแรม
   I'm going to the hotel.

Grammatical notes

1. Possessive adjectives (*khŏrng* + personal pronoun)

khŏrng (ของ) can be translated as "of" and it is used to
indicate the possession. As in the above example, *bâan
(khŏrng) khun* บ้าน (ของ) คุณ means "your house," or
more literally "house of you," and *khŏrng* (ของ) can be
omitted in a more informal context.

2. Future

The word *jà'* จะ (observe the glottal stop at the end, like
a *k*, but not written as such in Thai) indicates a future
tense, such as "will, going to, want to… ." In the above
examples, the English present continuous tense in the
translations contains this future meaning.

13   MÊUA-RÀI เมื่อไร when?

Khun jà' bpai mêua-rài? คุณจะไปเมื่อไร
When will you go?

→ *Phŏm jà' bpai wan níi.* ผมจะไปวันนี้
I'm going today.

→ *Chăn jà' bpai phrûng níi.* ฉันจะไปพรุ่งนี้
I'm going tomorrow.

Khun maa thĕung Grungthêhp mêua-rài?
คุณมาถึงกรุงเทพเมื่อไร
When did you arrive in Bangkok?

→ *Mêua waan níi.* เมื่อวานนี้ **Yesterday.**

→ *Athít thîi láew.* อาทิตย์ที่แล้ว **Last week.**

→ *Wan Phút.* วันพุธ **On Wednesday.**

Mêua-rài khun jà maa? เมื่อไรคุณจะมา
When will you come?

14   THAM-MAI ทำไม why?

Khun maa Chiang Mai tham-mai?
คุณมาเชียงใหม่ทำไม
Why have you come to Chiang Mai?

→ *Maa thîau.* มาเที่ยว
On holiday (for leisure, recreation).

→ *Maa thurá'.* มาธุระ **On business.**

Tham-mai maa cháa? ทำไมมาช้า
Why did you come late?

→ *Rót dtìt.* รถติด **There was a traffic jam.**

→ *Fŏn dtòk mâak.* ฝนตกมาก
There was heavy rain.

→ *Chăn dtèun săai.* ฉันตื่นสาย **I woke up late.**

15 PHRÓ WÂA' เพราะว่า because, as

Tham-mai khun mâi maa? ทำไมคุณไม่มา
Why didn't you come?

→ *Phró' wâa leum.* เพราะว่าลืม
Because I forgot.

Rau jamdâi, phró' wâa sămkhan mâak.
เราจำได้ เพราะว่า สำคัญมาก
We remembered, because it is very important.

Jambpen dtông séu khâau, phró' wâa jà' mòt.
จำเป็นต้องซื้อข้าวเพราะว่าจะหมด
It's necessary to buy some rice, as it's going to run out.

Khun khruu dù', phró' wâa dèk-dèk son.
คุณครูดุเพราะว่าเด็กๆซน
The teacher was cross because the children were naughty.

16 YANG-NGAI (informal)/YANG-RAI (formal)
ยังไง **how?**

Khun maa thîi nîi yang-ngai? คุณมาที่นี่ยังไง
How did you get here?

→ *Maa taxi.* มาแท็กซี่ **I came by taxi.**

Phŏm jà' bpai Ayutthaya yang-ngai?
ผมจะไปอยุธยายังไง
How do I get to Ayutthaya?

→ *Bpai thaang reua.* ไปทางเรือ **By boat.**

→ *Bpai rót yon.* ไปรถยนต์ **By car.**

Gin yang-ngai? กินยังไง **How do I eat it?**

→ *Chái chórn.* ใช้ช้อน **With a spoon.**

→ *Chái dta-gìap.* ใช้ตะเกียบ **With chopsticks.**

NOTE: The word *chái* ใช้ is actually a verb, meaning "to use," but in some places can better be translated as "with, using."

17 KHRAI? ใคร **who?**

Khău bpen khrai? เพำทนอำ หยฟแนใคร
Who is she/he?

→ *Khău bpen phêuan.* เขาเป็นเพื่อน
She/he's a friend.

Khrai phûut khá? ใครพูดคะ
Who's speaking? (on the telephone) (woman asking)

→ *Sŏmmăi phûut.* สมหมายพูด
This is Sommai (speaking).

Khrai bòrk khun? ใครบอกคุณ **Who told you?**

→ *Hŭa nâa bòrk.* หัวหน้าบอก **The boss told me.**

Khun bpai shopping gàp khrai?
คุณไปชอปปิ้งกับใคร
Who are you going shopping with?

→ *Bpai gàp Nók.* ไปกับนก **I'm going with Nok.**

Grammatical notes

Some question words such as "when," "why," "who" do
not always have to be placed at the end of the sentence.
They can be put at the beginning as well.

18 THÂU-RAI? เท่าไร how much?

Nîi thâu-rai? นี่เท่าไร **How much is this?**

An nîi thâu-rai? อันนี้เท่าไร
How much does this one cost?

Khun aayú' thâu-rai? คุณอายุเท่าไร
How old are you?

→ *Chăn aayú' hòk-sìp bpii.* ฉันอายุ 60 ปี
  I'm (aged) sixty.

Naan thâu-rai? นานเท่าไร
How long (will it take)?

→ *Bpra-maan sŏng chûa-mong.*
  ประมาณสองชั่วโมง
  Approximately two hours.

Jàak sanăam-bin bpai rong-raem, naan thâu-rai?
จากสนามบินไปโรงแรมนานเท่าไร
**How long does it take to get from the airport to
the hotel?**

→ *Rau-rau khrêung chûamong.*
  ราวราวครึ่งชั่วโมง **About half an hour.**

Numerals

The system of numerals is quite regular, but has some
unexpected terms. It works as follows:

1	*nèung*	หนึ่ง
2	*sŏng*	สอง
3	*săam*	สาม
4	*sìi*	สี่
5	*hâa*	ห้า
6	*hòk*	หก

7	*jèt*	เจ็ด
8	*bàet*	แปด
9	*gâau*	เก้า
10	*sìp*	สิบ
11	*sìp-èt*	สิบเอ็ด
12	*sìp-sŏng*	สิบสอง
13	*sìp-săam*	สิบสาม
14	*sìp-sìi*	สิบสี่
15	*sìp-hâa*	สิบห้า
16	*sìp-hòk*	สิบหก
17	*sìp-jèt*	สิบเจ็ด
18	*sìp-bàet*	สิบแปด
19	*sìp-gâau*	สิบเก้า
20	*yîi-sìp* [not *"sŏng-sìp"*!]	ยี่สิบ
21	*yîi-sìp-èt*	ยี่ สิบ เอ็ด
22	*yîi-sìp-sŏng*	ยี่สิบสอง
23	*yîi-sìp-săam*	ยี่สิบสาม
30	*săam-sìp*	สามสิบ
40	*sìi-sìp*	สี่สิบ
50	*hâa-sìp*	ห้าสิบ

60	*hòk-sìp*	หกสิบ
70	*jèt-sìp*	เจ็ดสิบ
80	*bàet-sìp*	แปดสิบ
90	*gâau-sìp*	เก้าสิบ
100	*róoi*	หนึ่งร้อย or ร้อย
200	*sŏng róoi*	สองร้อย
300	*săam róoi*	สามร้อย
400	*sìi róoi*	สี่ร้อย
500	*hâa róoi*	ห้าร้อย
600	*hòk róoi*	หก ร้อย
700	*jèt róoi*	เจ็ดร้อย
800	*bàet róoi*	แปดร้อย
900	*gâau róoi*	เก้าร้อย
1,000	*phan*	หนึ่งพัน or พัน
2,000	*sŏng phan*	สองพัน
3,000	*săam phan*	สามพัน etc.,
10,000	*mèun*	หนึ่งหมื่น or หมื่น
20,000	*sŏng mèun*	สองหมื่น etc.
100,000	*săen*	แสน
300,000	*săam săen*	สามแสน etc.

| 1,000,000 | *láan* | หนึ่งล้าน or ล้าน |
| 4,000,000 | *sìi láan* | สี่ล้าน etc. |

It is important to memorize these large units, as they do not follow the Western system of "ten thousand" or "one hundred thousand."

NOTE: In order to make an ordinal number, we just use the word *thîi* ที่ in front of the cardinal number, e.g. *thîi hâa* ที่ ห้า, "fifth."

19 GÌI? กี่ how many?

Gìi khon? กี่คน **How many people?**

Khun mii lûuk gìi khon? คุณมีลูกกี่คน
How many children do you have?

Gìi bàht? กี่บาท
How many baht (how much does it cost)?

→ *Róoi hâa-sìp bàht.* 150 บาท
   One hundred and fifty baht.

Gìi chûa-mong? กี่ชั่วโมง **How many hours?**

Pai Chiang Mai gìi chûa-mong?
ไปเชียงใหม่กี่ชั่วโมง
How many hours is it to Chiang Mai?

Gìi wan? กี่วัน **How many days?**

Gìi deuan? กี่เดือน **How many months?**

Gìi bpii? กี่ปี **How many years?**

Grammatical note

In Thai, a classifier is used when counting items or referring to numbers of items. Each object has a specific classifier word that should be used when you are stating the
quantity of that object. For example, '*khon*' is used when
counting people. The basic pattern with classifier is:

noun + number/quantity + classifier	
นักศึกษา 2 คน *nák-sùek-săa săwng khon*	two students [lit. students + two + classifier]
แมว 3 ตัว *maew săam tua*	three cats [lit. cats + three + classifier]

The word *an* อัน can also serve as a kind of neutral classifier, if you don't happen to know the right one, e.g. *gìi
an?* กี่ อัน how many "things"?

GÔR DÂI ก็ได้ any- (please yourself)

Khun jà' gin à-rai? คุณจะกินอะไร
What are you going to eat?

→ *Arai gôr dâi!* อะไรก็ได้
Anything! (Whatever you like, I don't mind)

Yùt thîi nǎi? หยุดที่ไหน **Where will we stop?**

→ *Thîi nǎi gôr dâi.* ที่ไหนก็ได้.
Anywhere you like.

Mêua-rai òrk jàak hông níi?
เมื่อไรออกจากห้องนี้
What time do we leave this room?

→ *Mêua-rai gôr dâi* เมื่อไรก็ได้
Any time (at your convenience).

Khrai jà' bpai séu ahǎan? ใครจะไปซื้ออาหาร
Who's going to buy the food?

→ *Khrai gôr dâi.* ใครก็ได้
Anybody (it doesn't matter).

Ordering a meal

21 **HĬU** หิว **hungry**

Khun hĭu mái? คุณหิวไหม **Are you hungry?**

→ *Hĭu nít nòi.* หิวนิดหน่อย **A bit hungry.**

→ *Hĭu mâak.* หิวมาก **Very hungry.**

→ *Mâi hĭu.* ไม่หิว **I'm not hungry.**

Hĭu náam. หิวน้ำ **I'm thirsty.**
(literally "hungry for water").

Hĭu khâao. หิวข้าว
I want something to eat (literally "hungry for
rice"—rice represents food in general, as it is the
most important food).

22 **YÀAK** อยาก **want to, would like to...**

Phŏm yàak gin ahăan Thai.
ผมอยากกินอาหารไทย
I would like to eat (some) Thai food.

Chăn yàak bpai Siam Square.
ฉันอยากไปสยามสแควร์
I would like to go to Siam Square.

Rau yàak gin thîi ráan rim. เราอยากกินที่ร้านริมน้ำ
We would like to eat (have a meal) at a restaurant on the edge of the river.

Khău yàak gin nai reua. เขาอยากกินในเรือ
He/she wants to eat on (Thai: **in**) **the boat.**

Phŏm mâi yàak gin bia. ผมไม่อยากกินเบียร์
I don't want to drink (Thai: **"eat"!**) **beer.**

23 KHŎR ขอ may I have...? (polite request)

Khŏr menu. ขอเมนู **May I have the menu?**

Khŏr khâao nèung môr. ขอข้าว 1 หม้อ
May I have one pot of rice?

Khŏr gaeng sŏng thîi. ขอแกง 2 ที่
May I have two servings of curry? (literally "curry two places")

Khŏr náam săam gâeu. ขอน้ำ 3 แก้ว
May I have three glasses of water?

Khŏr Pepsi sìi khwàt. ขอเป๊ปซี่ 4 ขวด
May I have four bottles of Pepsi?

Khŏr gaafae hâa thûay. ขอกาแฟ 5 ถ้วย
May I have five cups of coffee?

Also:

Khŏr thôot. ขอโทษ
I beg your pardon (excuse me, sorry).

24   AU เอา   I want; bring me; I'll take...

Phŏm au dtôm yam gûng nèung thîi.
ผมเอาต้มยำกุ้ง 1 ที่
I want one serving of "tom yam gung" (spicy prawn soup).

Chăn au khâao phàt nèung jaan.
ฉันเอาข้าวผัด 1 จาน
I want a (one) plate of fried rice.

Khun au bia mái? คุณเอาเบียร์ไหม
Do you want beer?

→ *Mâi au!* ไม่เอา   **No, I don't.**
   (Note repetition of the verb in this answer.)

→ *Au Pepsi.* เอาเป๊ปซี่   **I 'll have a Pepsi.**

Khun au náam khěng dûai mái?
คุณเอาน้ำแข็งด้วยไหม
Will you have ice with that?

  → *Au dûai.* เอาด้วย **Yes, I will.**

Au náam chaa rěu gaafae? เอาน้ำชาหรือกาแฟ
Will you have tea or coffee?

  → *Au náam chaa.* เอาน้ำชา **I'll have tea.**

Au ìik! เอาอีก **I want another/more!**

25 SÀI ใส่ to add, put something in

Sài nom nít nòi. ใส่นมนิดหน่อย
With a little milk in it.

Sài nám-dtaan nít nòi. ใส่น้ำตาลนิดหน่อย
With a little sugar in it.

Mâi sài nom. ไม่ใส่นม **Without milk.**

Mâi sài nám-dtaan. ไม่ใส่น้ำตาล **Without sugar.**

NOTE: the verb *sài* ใส่ has various meanings: "to insert; to wear (clothes)."

26 CHÔRP ชอบ to like, have a liking for

Phǒm chôrp gaeng néua. ผมชอบแกงเนื้อ
I like beef curry.

Khǎu chôrp dtôm yam gûng mâak.

เขาชอบต้มยำกุ้งมาก

She likes "tom yam gung" soup very much.

Faràng mâi chôrp thurian, měn mâak.

ฝรั่งไม่ชอบทุเรียน, เหม็นมาก

Foreigners don't like durian—it's very smelly.

Chǎn chôrp phèt. ฉันชอบเผ็ด

I like it hot (hot food).

Chǎn chôrp thúk yaang. ฉันชอบทุกอย่าง

I like any kind (of food).

Khun Manát chôrp bplaa mâak gwàa gài.

คุณมนัสชอบปลามากกว่าไก่

Mr Manat likes fish more than chicken.

NOTE: We use *gwàa* กว่า to say "more" (*-er*) when making a comparison, e.g. *dii gwàa* ดีกว่า, "better."

27 PHÈT เผ็ด hot (spicy)

Khun chôrp phèt mái? คุณชอบเผ็ดไหม

Do you like hot food?

→ *Chôrp phèt nít nòi.* ชอบเผ็ดนิดหน่อย
   I like it a bit hot.

→ *Chôrp phèt bpaan-glaang.* ชอบเผ็ดปานกลาง
   I like it medium hot.

→ *Chôrp phèt mâak.* ชอบเผ็ดมาก
I like it very hot.

→ *Mâi chôrp phèt leui.* ไม่ชอบเผ็ดเลย
I don't like it hot at all.

Gaeng gài nîi phèt mâak. แกงไก่นี้เผ็ดมาก
This chicken curry is very hot.

Gaeng bplaa mâi khôi phèt. แกงปลาไม่ค่อยเผ็ด
The fish curry isn't very hot.

Náam jîm phèt mâak-mâak! น้ำจิ้มเผ็ดมากมาก
The sauce (dip) is very, very hot!

28 ARÒI อร่อย delicious, tasty, nice

Ahǎan Thai aròi mái? อาหารไทยอร่อยไหม
Is Thai food tasty?

→ *Aròi mâak!* อร่อยมาก It's very delicious!

Gaeng phèt gài, aròi mái? แกงเผ็ดไก่อร่อยไหม
Is the spicy chicken curry tasty?

Gaeng mǔu aròi gwàa gaeng gài.
แกงหมูอร่อยกว่าแกงไก่
The pork curry is tastier than the chicken.

Gaeng néua aròi thîi-sùt. แกงเนื้ออร่อยที่สุด
The beef curry is the tastiest (of all).

NOTE: we can say "the most" (*-est*) using the word *thîi-sùt* ที่สุด placed after an adjective, as above.

29 ÌM อิ่ม full; to have had enough

Ìm mái? อิ่มไหม **Have you had enough?**

- → *Ìm láew.* อิ่มแล้ว
  Yes, I have (literally "already full").
- → *Yang mâi ìm.* ยังไม่อิ่ม
  Not yet (I'd like some more).
- → *Ìm mâak!* อิ่มมาก **I'm very full!**

30 AHǍAN อาหาร food, meal

NOTE: the spelling in Thai is *aahǎan* อาหาร, but the first "a" is pronounced short.

ahǎan Thai อาหารไทย **Thai food**

ahǎan cháau อาหารเช้า **breakfast**

ahǎan thîang อาหารเที่ยง **lunch**

ahǎan yen อาหารเย็น **dinner**

ahǎan khâm อาหารค่ำ **supper**

Cultural note

Table etiquette in Thailand

Most visitors to Thailand look forward to enjoying Thai food, which is justly famous for its delicious flavors, produced with interesting sauces and herbs—not just chillis! This food can be found in many good restaurants (*ráan ahǎan*) ร้านอาหาร and hotels, but do be cautious about eating from the many roadside stalls, as they may not be very clean, and the noise of the traffic in the street is a nuisance too.

Thai food is eaten with a spoon and fork, but Chinese dishes such as noodles can better be eaten with chopsticks, which take some practice to use. When passing or receiving food, use your right hand, as the left is considered as less polite. It is also important not to reach over or stand over someone's head, as this is regarded as a space not to be intruded on.

The most senior (oldest) people present are served first, and the younger ones help them. Wait till the others have been served before beginning.

The rice is regarded as the main part of the meal. The other dishes are mere auxiliaries added to it, and so are termed *gàp-khâao* กับข้าว, literally "with the rice." Take your rice first, and then add other things to it. Do not dip your own spoon into the common dish if you are sharing it with the others.

It is best to take plain water (*nám bplàau* น้ำเปล่า) with your meal. The custom is to drink after you have finished eating, rather than during the meal. To relieve the burning taste of too many chillis, just take some more plain rice. Fruit may be served to finish up and freshen the mouth.

To call a waiter (more likely a waitress) (*khon serp* คนเสริพ, from English "serve"), just raise your hand. If you beckon, do it with the fingers down, not up. Thais will address the waiter with *nóng* น้อง ("younger brother/sister"), but foreigners may not feel comfortable with this.

Cheun khráp. เชิญครับ
Please go ahead (literally "I invite you").

Shopping and negotiating

31 **SÉU** ซื้อ **to buy**

Khun jà' séu à-rai? คุณจะซื้ออะไร
What do you want to buy?

Phǒm/chǎn jà' séu <u>gaang-geng</u>.
ผม ฉัน จะ ซื้อ <u>กางเกง</u> **I want to buy <u>pants</u>.**

Substitute the noun underlined:

sêua เสื้อ **blouse, shirt**

sêua yêut เสื้อยืด **a T-shirt**

gra-bprong กระโปรง **a skirt**

nek tai เนคไท **a tie**

phâa mǎi ผ้าไหม **silk cloth**

phâa fâai ผ้าฝ้าย **cotton cloth**

chút norn ชุดนอน **pyjamas**

gaang-geng กางเกง **pants**

grà-pǎo กระเป๋า **purse, bag**

rawng-tháo รองเท้า **shoes**

thǔng-tháo ถุงเท้า **socks**

gradàat thít-chûu กระดาษทิชชู่
toilet paper (not "tissue paper"!)

sabùu สบู่ **soap**

yaa sǐi fan ยาสีฟัน **toothpaste**

chaempuu แชมพู **shampoo**

bpâeng แป้ง **powder**

Séu rorng-tháau thîi nǎi? ซื้อรองเท้าที่ไหน
Where do we buy shoes?

- → *Thîi dtalàat.* ที่ตลาด **In the market.**

- → *Thîi hâang.* ที่ ห้าง
  In a department store.

- → *Thîi supermarket.* ที่ซูเปอร์มาเก็ต
  In a supermarket.

- → *Thîi chán sǎam.* ที่ชั้นสาม **On the third floor.**

32 LÓT ลด **to reduce, lower**

Lót dâi mái? ลดได้ไหม
Can you lower the price?

- → *Lót mâi dâi.* ลดไม่ได้ **I can't reduce it!**

- → *Lót dâi nít nòi.* ลดได้นิดหน่อย
  I can reduce it a bit.

- → *Lót láew.* ลดแล้ว **I've already reduced it!**

Thîi supermarket lót mâi dâi.
ที่ซุปเปอร์มาเก็ตลดไม่ได้
Prices can't be reduced in a supermarket.

Cultural note

It is quite acceptable to bargain in any market in Thailand—the Thais expect it. One method is to halve the seller's starting price, and then come up half of the difference. The result should then be very reasonable. The prices charged to foreigners are always higher than for the locals, so if you can get some reduction you've done well. But don't try it in a supermarket or department store, of course.

34 NÒI DÂI-MÁI หน่อยได้ไหม Would you please?/Could you please?/ May I?/Please...

Lót nòi dâi mái? ลดหน่อยได้ไหม
Could you please lower the price?

Lót ìik nòi dâi mái? ลดอีกหน่อยได้ไหม
Could you lower it a bit more?

Khǒr lorng nòi dâi mái? ขอลองหน่อยได้ไหม
Could I try it on?

Khŏr doo sêua nòi dâi mái?
ขอดูเสื้อตัวนั้นหน่อยได้ไหม
May I look at that shirt?

Khŏr gaafae rórn nòi dâi mái.
ขอกาแฟร้อนหน่อยได้ไหม
Could I have some hot coffee, please?

Grammatical note

Nòi หน่อย (*lit.* a little bit) and *dâi mái* ได้ไหม (*lit.* "Could you?") can be used separately to make a request by adding one of them at the end of a sentence. However, you can strengthen the degree of politeness by using the combination of *nòi dâi mái* หน่อยได้ไหม.

34 KHANÀAT ขนาด size; SĬI สี color

Khanàat năi? ขนาดไหน **Which size?**

NOTE: *Năi* ไหน suggests a choice out of many possible ones; *à-rai* อะไร "what?" could not be used here.

- → *Khanàat lék.* ขนาดเล็ก **Small (size).**

- → *Khanàat glaang.* ขนาดกลาง **Medium (size).**

- → *Khanàat yài.* ขนาดใหญ่ **Large.**

- → *Khanàat ber bàet.* ขนาดเบอร์แปด
  Size (number) 8.

Sĭi à-rai? สีอะไร **What color?**

- → *Sĭi dam* สีดำ **Black**
- → *Sĭi daeng* สีแดง **Red**
- → *Sĭi khăau* สีขาว **White**
- → *Sĭi khăau* สีเขียว **Green**
- → *Sĭi nám-ngoen* สีน้ำเงิน **Navy blue**
- → *Sĭi fáa* สีฟ้า **Light blue**
- → *Sĭi lŭeang* สีเหลือง **Yellow**
- → *Sĭi sôm* สีส้ม **Orange**
- → *Sĭi chom-phou* สีชมพู **Pink**
- → *Sĭi mûang* สีม่วง **Purple**
- → *Sĭi nám-taan* สีน้ำตาล **Brown**

NOTE: We repeat the word *sĭi* สี before specifying the color.

35 MII มี to have, there is/are

Mii (sêua) sĭi fáa mái? มีเสื้อสีฟ้าไหม
Do you have (a) blue (shirt)?

Mii khanàat yài mái? มีขนาดใหญ่ไหม
Do you have a bigger size?

Mii dtôm yam gûng mái? มีต้มยำกุ้งไหม
Do you have "tom yam gung" (spicy soup with shrimp)?

PHA-NÀEK แผนก department, section

pha-nàek sêua phâa แผนกเสื้อผ้า
clothing department

pha-nàek rohng táu แผนกรองเท้า
shoe department

pha-nàek grabpǎu แผนกกระเป๋า
bag department

Pha-nàek sêua-phâa yùu thîi nǎi?
แผนกเสื้อผ้าอยู่ที่ไหน
Where is the clothing department?

→ *Yùu chán sìi.* อยู่ชั้นสี่
On the fourth floor (literally, "floor four").

KHǍAI ขาย to sell

Khǎai gài yâang. ขายไก่ย่าง
We sell roast chicken.

Rau khǎai komputêr. เราขายคอมพิวเตอร์
We sell computers.

Rau khǎai bplìik. เราขายปลีก **We sell retail.**

Rau khǎai sòng. เราขายส่ง **We sell wholesale.**

Khít raakhaa khǎai sòng. คิดราคาขายส่ง
Charge (calculate) your wholesale price.

Khít raakhaa khon Thai. คิดราคาคนไทย
Charge the local price (for Thai people).

JÀAI ขาย **to pay**

Phǒm jàai ngeun sòt. ผมจ่ายเงินสด **I'll pay cash.**

Chǎn jàai dûai bàt kredit. ฉันจ่ายด้วยบัตรเครดิด
I'll pay by (with) credit card.

Rau jàai dûai chék. เราจ่ายด้วยเช็ค
We'll pay by cheque.

Khǎu jàai khròp/tháng-mòt. เขาจ่ายครบทั้งหมด
He pays (it) off completely.

→ *Jàai thii dîau.* จ่ายทีเดียว **In one go.**

→ *Jàai phon sòng.* จ่ายผ่อนส่ง
In installments.

→ *Jàai athit lá'nèung róoi bàht.*
จ่ายอาทิตย์ละร้อยบาท
100 baht per week (weekly).

→ *Jàai deuan lá' sìi róoi bàht.*
จ่ายเดือนละสี่ร้อยบาท
400 baht per month (monthly).

→ *Jàai bpii lá' hâa phan bàht.*
จ่ายปีละห้าพันบาท
5,000 baht per year (annually).

On the numerals, refer to pages 38–40.

39 CHÂU เช่า to rent, hire

Châu <u>rót</u>. เช่ารถ **To rent a car.**

Substitute the noun underlined:

modtersai มอเตอร์ไซค์ **a motorcycle**

bâan บ้าน **a house**

apartmen อพาร์ตเม็นท์ **an apartment**

kondo คอนโด; *hohng-chut* ห้องชุด **a condominium**

Châu rót raa-khaa thâu-rài? เช่ารถราคาเท่าไร
How much does it cost to rent a car?

→ *Athít lá' hâa róoi bàht.* อาทิตย์ละห้าร้อยบาท
500 baht per week.

→ *Deuan lá' sŏng phan bàht.*
เดือนละสองพันบาท
2,000 baht per month.

→ *Mèun sŏng phan bàht dtòr hòk deuan.*
หมื่นสองพันบาทต่อหกเดือน
12,000 baht for six months.

Compare also *mǎu rót* เหมารถ "to charter a car" (e.g. for group travel up-country).

40 KHÂA ค่า fare, rate, tariff

khâa châu ค่าเช่า rental rate

Khâa châu bâan thâu-rài? ค่าเช่าบ้านเท่าไร
How much is the rental of the house?

Khâa châu rót thâu-rài? ค่าเช่ารถเท่าไร
How much is the rental for a car?

Khâa taxi thâu-rài? ค่าแท็กซี่เท่าไร
How much is the taxi fare?

Getting about

41 BPAI ไป to go

Chăn jà bpai Chiang Mai yang-ngai?
ฉันจะไปเชียงใหม่ยังไง
How do I get to Chiang Mai?

→ *Bpai rót bas.* ไปรถบัส **By bus.**

→ *Bpai rót fai.* ไปรถไฟ **By train.**

→ *Bpai khrêuang bin.* ไปเครื่องบิน
   By plane.

Phŏm jà bpai Wat Phra Kaew yang-ngai?
ผมจะไปวัดพระแก้วยังไง
How do I get to the Emerald Buddha temple?

→ *Bpai rót fai fáa.* ไปรถไฟฟ้า **By skytrain.**

→ *Bpai rót may.* ไปรถเมล์ **By metro bus.**

→ *Bpai reua.* ไปเรือ **By boat.**

Mûea-waan-níi khun bpai năi maa?
เมื่อวานนี้คุณไปไหนมา
Where did you go yesterday?/Where have you been?

→ *Mûea-waan-níi chăn bpai ráan-aa-hăan.*
เมื่อวานนี้ฉันไปร้านอาหาร
Yesterday I went to the restaurant.

Phrûng-níi khun jà-bpai-năi? พรุ่งนี้คุณจะไปไหน
Where are you going tomorrow?

→ *Phrûng-níi phŏm jà bpai <u>thá-le</u>.*
พรุ่งนี้ผมจะไปทะเล
I'm going to the <u>beach</u> tomorrow.

Substitute the word underlined:

mâe-náam แม่น้ำ river

phuu-khao ภูเขา mountain

náam-tòk น้ำตก waterfall

rohng-phá-yaa-baan โรงพยาบาล hospital

rohng-năng โรงหนัง movie theater

rohng-raem โรงแรม hotel

rohng-rian โรงเรียน school

kli-nik คลีนิค clinic

sathăanii dtamruat สถานีตำรวจ police station

sathăanii rót fai สถานีรถไฟ train station

sathăan thûut สถานทูต embassy

hâang ห้าง department store

ráan-aa-hăan ร้านอาหาร restaurant

ráan-kaa-fae ร้านกาแฟ **coffee shop**

ráan-năng-sŭe ร้านหนังสือ **bookstore**

thá-na-khaan ธนาคาร **bank**

prai-sà-nii ไปรษณีย์ **post office**

má-hăa-wít-thá-yaa-lai มหาวิทยาลัย **university**

wát วัด **temple**

tàlàat ตลาด **market**

phí-phít-thá-phan พิพิธภัณฑ์ **museum**

ATM เอทีเอ็ม **automated teller machine**

Thá-na-khaan bpai thaang năi?
ธนาคารไปทางไหน
Which way/which direction to the bank?

→ *Bpai thaang sáai.* ไปทางซ้าย **Go to the left.**

→ *Deun dtrong bpai.* เดินตรงไป
Go straight ahead.

→ *Lîau khwăa.* เลี้ยวขวา **Turn right.**

→ *Bpai thaang níi.* ไปทางนี้ **Go this way.**

→ *Bpai thaang nán.* ไปทางนั้น **Go that way.**

Wát Pho bpai thaang năi? วัดโพธิ์ไปทางไหน
How do I get to Wat Pho?

→ *Bpai rót may săay 56.* ไปรถเมล์สาย 56
Take the bus number 56.

→ *Bpai rót taxi.* ไปรถแท็กซี่ **By taxi.**

NOTE: The word *năi* ไหน meaning "where" is usually used with the verb *bpai* "to go."

Grammatical note

Whether you talk about the past or the present, the form of the verb does not change in Thai. When talking about the future, the word *jà* can be placed in front of the verb, but this is not necessary.

Chăn bpai tàlàat. ฉันไปตลาด **I go to the market.**

Chăn bpai tàlàat. ฉันไปตลาด **I went to the market.**

Chăn (jà) bpai tàlàat. ฉัน(จะ)ไปตลาด
I'll go to the market.

42 KHÊUN ขึ้น to go up, ascend; to get on (a mode of transport); to increase, get better

Khêun rót fai thîi năi? ขึ้นรถไฟที่ไหน
Where do you get on the train?

→ *Thîi Hŭa-lampong.* ที่หัวลำโพง
  At Hualampong (Bangkok's main station)

→ *Thîi sathăanii rót fai.* ที่สถานีรถไฟ
  At the station.

Khêun bandai. ขึ้นบันได **To go up the stairs.**

Khêun chán bon. ขึ้นชั้นบน
To go (up) to the upper level.

Khêun chán bon-sùt. ขึ้นชั้นบนสุด
To go to the very top.

Khêun líp bpai chán sìp. ขึ้นลิฟท์ไปชั้นสิบ
To take the lift to level 10.

Dii khêun. ดีขึ้น **To get (become) better.**

Tham hâi piǔ khǎau khêun. ทำให้ผิวขาวขึ้น
It gives you whiter skin.

(Note the word order in these last two examples.)

43 LONG ลง to go down; to get off (a mode of transport)

Phǒm long rót thîi Siam Square.
ผมลงรถที่สยามสแควร์
I get (got) off the bus at Siam Square.

Chǎn long rót fai thîi sathǎanii Sǎmsěn.
ฉันลงรถไฟที่สถานีสามเสน
I get (got) off the train at Samsen Station.

Rau long rót bas thîi sathǎan thûut Australia.
เราลงรถบัสที่สถานทูตออสเตรเลีย
We get off the bus at the Australian embassy.

Khǎu long rót taxi thîi Sǔansàt Dusit.
เขาลงรถแท็กซี่ที่สวนสัตว์ดุสิต
He got out of the taxi at Dusit Zoo.

Khǎu long khrêuang bin thîi Phuket.
เขาลงเครื่องบินที่ภูเก็ต
She got off the plane in Phuket.

BUT

Chǎn long reua thîi Thammasat.
ฉันลงเรือที่ธรรมศาสตร์
I got on the boat at Thammasat.

NOTE: This is an exception—you have to step down to
get on the boat. And to get off you have to *khêun fàng*
ขึ้นฝั่ง, "climb the bank"!

44 JORNG จอง to book, reserve

Phǒm jorng thîi nâng sǎam thîi. ผมจองที่นั่งสามที่
I booked three seats.

Chǎn jorng dtǔa sǎam thîi. ฉันจองตั๋วสามที่
I reserved three tickets.

NOTE: In these two examples, the word *thîi* ที่ ("place")
serves as a counting word for seats or tickets. These
could be on a bus, train, plane or even in a restaurant or
at a seminar.

Rau jà' jorng hông nèung hông.
เราจะจองห้องหนึ่งห้อง
We want to book one room.

NOTE: Again, the second *hông* ห้อง is a classifier for rooms.

Hông dîau ห้องเดี่ยว **a single room,** or

Hông khûu ห้องคู่ **a double room (room for two),**

or you could say

Dtiang dîau เตียงเดี่ยว **a single bed,** or

Dtiang khûu เตียงคู่ **a double bed.**

45 GLAI ไกล **far;** GLÂI ใกล้ **close**

Because these two words have opposite meanings and only a different tone to distinguish them in pronunciation, they are listed together here. Note the word order in the examples below.

Jàak Grungthêhp bpai Ayutthia glai mái?
จากกรุงเทพไปอยุธยาไกลไหม
Is it far from Bangkok to Ayutthia?

→ *Glai mâak.* ไกลมาก **It's a long way.**

Glai mâak khâe-nǎi? ไกลมากแค่ไหน **How far?**

Glai gìi giloh? ไกลกี่กิโล **How many kilometers?**

→ *Rau-rau róoi giloh.* ราวราวร้อยกิโล
   About a hundred kilometers.

Jàak Grungthêhp bpai Phuket glai mái?
จากกรุงเทพไปภูเก็ตไกลไหม
It is far from Bangkok to Phuket?

→ *Glai mâak.* ไกลมาก **It's a very long way.**

→ *Gìi giloh?* กี่กิโล **How many kilometers?**

→ *Mâi rúu.* ไม่รู้ **I don't know.**

→ *Mâi sâap.* ไม่ทราบ **I don't know.** (more
   formal/polite)

7-Eleven yùu glai mái?
เซเว่นอีเลฟเว่นอยู่ไกลไหม
Is 7-Eleven far from here?

→ *Glâi.* ใกล้ **It's close.**

→ *Glâi mâak.* ใกล้มาก **It's very close.**

→ *Deun bpai dâi.* เดินไปได้ **You can walk.**

→ *Deun sìp-hâa nathii.* เดินสิบห้านาที
   It's a 15-minute walk.

→ *Khêun rót hâa nathii.* ขึ้นรถห้านาที
   It's 5 minutes by car.

THÀNǑN ถนน road;
SOI ซอย side-street, alley

Sathǎan-thûut Australia yùu thîi nǎi?
สถานทูตออสเตรเลียอยู่ที่ไหน
Where is the Australian embassy?

Thànǒn à-rai? ที่ถนนอะไร **On what road?**

→ *Thîi thànǒn Sathorn dtâi.* ที่ถนนสาทรใต้
  On South Sathorn Road.

Rong-raem Mandarin yùu thîi nǎi?
โรงแรมแมนดารินอยู่ที่ไหน
Where is the Mandarin Hotel?

→ *Thîi thànǒn Phra Ram 4.* ที่ถนนพระรามสี่
  On Rama Road 4.

NOTE: The term *thànǒn* ถนน normally refers to a main
road. On each side of a main city road (which may be
very long) we have numbered side-streets, odd on one
side and even on the other, called *soi*. So when looking
for an address it's important to note which *soi* ซอย, and
the house number within it. House numbers often have a
slash (*tháp* ทับ), e.g. 334/5.

khâam thànǒn ข้ามถนน **to cross the road**

deun dtaam thànǒn เดินตามถนน
to follow the road

glaang thànǒn กลางถนน
the middle of the road

47 KHÂNG ข้าง side

khâng nâa ข้างหน้า **the front**

khâng lăng ข้างหลัง **the back**

khâng bon ข้างบน **upstairs**

khâng lâang ข้างล่าง **downstairs**

BUT for left and right

thaang sáai ทางซ้าย **(on the) left-hand side**

thaang kwăa ทางขวา **(on the) right-hand side**

48 THĚUNG ถึง to reach, arrive at

Bpai thěung Phuket dton-năi?
ไปถึงภูเก็ตตอนไหน
When do we get to Phuket?

Chái wehlaa deun thaang sǒng chûamong.
ใช้เวลาเดินทาง 2 ชั่วโมง
It takes two hours to get there.

Rau maa thĕung bâan wan Jan.
เรามาถึงบ้านวันจันทร์
We arrive home on Monday.

bpai thĕung dtrong wehlaa ไปถึงตรงเวลา
to arrive on time

bpai thĕung săi ไปถึงสาย **to arrive late**

bpai thĕung cháa ไปถึงช้า **to arrive late (behind time)**

JANGWÀT จังหวัด province (a common spelling is Changwat)

49

bpai dtàang jangwàt ไปต่างจังหวัด
to go up-country (into the provinces, away from the capital)

Jangwàt Grabii [Krabii] mii chaihàat sŭay mâak.
จังหวัดกระบี่มีชายหาดสวยมาก
Krabii Province has very beautiful beaches.

Jangwàt Surin mii cháang maak.
จังหวัดสุรินทร์มีช้างมาก
Surin Province has lots of elephants.

Jangwàt Chiangrai mii phukhău sŭung.
จังหวัดเชียงรายมีภูเขาสูง
Chiangrai Province has high mountains.

Jangwàt Chiang Mai mii aagàat dii.
จังหวัดเชียงใหม่มีอากาศดี
Chiang Mai Province has a good climate.

NOTE: A province is divided into districts, termed *ampheu*
อำเภอ (also spelled *amphur*) and sub-districts termed
dtambon ตำบล (or *tambon*). Below these is the lowest
level—the village, *mùu-bâan* หมู่บ้าน.

50 WÁT วัด temple

Wát Phrá' Gâeo วัดพระแก้ว
Temple of the Emerald Buddha (in central Bangkok)

Wát Phoh วัดโพธิ์ **Temple of the Reclining Buddha**

Wát Baworn วัดบวร (also spelled Bovornives)
**famous as seat of the Supreme Patriarch and for its
teaching and meditation program**

Wát Arun วัดอรุณ **Temple of the Dawn**

Wát Phrá' Sĭi Mahǎathâat วัดพระศรีมหาธาตุ
**name of the oldest temple in Nakhorn Si Thammarat
in southern Thailand**

Wat Phráthâat Doi Suthêhp พระธาตุดอยสุเทพ
name of the most famous temple in Chiang Mai

Cultural note

Thailand has thousands of Buddhist temples. This is because it is a Buddhist country. The kind of Buddhism is the same as that of Sri Lanka, Burma and Cambodia, that is, Theravada. The clergy (monks) wear distinctive yellow, orange or reddish brown robes and have shaven heads.

There are several large and famous temples in Bangkok that foreign visitors are often taken to see. You can admire the architecture and ornaments. There are also lesser known temples in the city that are worth seeing. Feel free to drop in—nobody will accost you! However, you are expected to observe the same rules as Thais do:

- remove your shoes before entering a building (the place to leave them will be clear, and is quite safe);
- dress respectfully—cover up the thighs and chest;
- if sitting on the floor, never point the feet in the direction of a Buddha image; and
- do not touch or climb on any Buddha image (photos are okay).

Thais are extremely sensitive about any intended or unintended disrespect toward the Buddhist religion, including Buddha images, large and small, because they are regarded as filled with sacred power (*saksit* ศักดิ์สิทธิ์).

By all means chat with a monk, if he wants to practice his English! You should greet him with a *waai* ไหว้, but he will not return it. (Monks only make a *waai* ไหว้

to their superiors.) A woman must never touch a monk, even his robe. This includes giving or receiving an object—it has to be put down first. This is because monks follow a very strict set of rules of life (called the **Vinaya** วินัย), which include chastity (not marrying or having any contact with females). They also never eat after midday, until the next morning, when they go out to collect alms in their bowl.

Supporting monks with donations of food, and similar acts of generosity, brings us religious merit (**bun** บุญ), which will help create good conditions for us in this life and the next. You may be interested to pick up a simple handbook of Buddhist belief and practice, including for example the Five Precepts:

1. I undertake the training in abstention from killing living beings;

2. I undertake the training in abstention from taking what is not given;

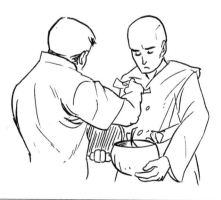

3. I undertake the training in abstention from acts of sexual misconduct;
4. I undertake the training in abstention from false speech;
5. I undertake the training in abstention from using any intoxication substance.

You will see that these are not formulated as "commandments," but are intended as guidelines for mindfulness, leading to wisdom. But by no means all Thai people stick strictly to these precepts!

The monks spend most of their time in the temple, where they chant (in Pali, the ancient language of the Buddha), hold ceremonies, preach to the lay people, study, or are available for consultation. They also go out, when invited, to hold ceremonies with chanting such as a house-warming in order to convey blessings for a new home or business. Some monks teach ethics in schools. Others devote their lives to contemplation and meditation.

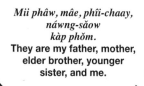

Family and friends

51 **PHÔR** พ่อ **father**

Khun phôr tham ngaan thîi opfít.
พ่อทำงานที่ออฟฟิศ
Father is working at the office.

Khun phôr ayú' thâu-rai? คุณพ่ออายุเท่าไร
How old is (your) father?

→ *Khun phôr ayú' hâa-sìp bpii.* คุณพ่ออายุ 50 ปี
Father is fifty years old.

Khun mâe yùu thîi năi? คุณแม่อยู่ที่ไหน
Where does your mother live?

→ *Thîi Isăan, jangwàt Khon-gaen.*
ที่อีสานจังหวัดขอนแก่น
In the Northeast, Khon-gaen Province.

NOTES

1. The title *khun* คุณ is put before kinship terms, as
   here, to indicate respect, either for one's own father
   or someone else's. The same applies to mother, uncle
   or aunt. The translation "Mr" or "Mrs" clearly does
   not apply.

2. *Isăan* อีสาน is one of the six regions of Thailand. The name means "northeast." These regions, termed *phâak* ภาค, are not official divisions, however, as is the case with the province.

Other terms:

phôr dtaa พ่อตา **father-in-law (wife's father)**

phôr phŭa พ่อผัว **father-in-law (husband's father)**

phôr săamii พ่อสามี **father-in-law** (more formal/polite)

phôr bâan พ่อบ้าน **head of the household**

phôr líang พ่อเลี้ยง **step-father.**

52 MÂE แม่ mother

Khun mâe tham ahăan nai khrua.
คุณแม่ทำอาหารในครัว
Mother is cooking in the kitchen.

Mâe au khayá' bpai thíng. แม่เอาขยะไปทิ้ง
Mother takes the rubbish out (to throw away).

Mâe bâan sák phâa. แม่บ้านซักผ้า
The housekeeper is washing clothes.

mâe phŭa แม่ผัว **mother-in-law (husband's mother)**

mâe yaai แม่ยาย **mother-in-law (wife's mother)**

mâe líang แม่เลี้ยง **step-mother**

phôr-mâe พ่อแม่ **parents (father and mother)**

Phôr-mâe rák lûuk. พ่อแม่รักลูก
Parents love their children.

Phôr-mâe mii lûuk sŏng khon. พ่อแม่มีลูกสองคน
My parents have two children.

Phôr-mâe sĭa chiiwít láew. พ่อแม่เสียชีวิตแล้ว
My parents are deceased (have passed away).

NOTE: The expression *sĭa chiiwít* เสียชีวิต (literally "to lose one's life") is respectful or formal; contrast plain *dtai* ตาย, "to die."

---

53 **PHÎI** พี่ **older sibling** (brother or sister);
NÓNG น้อง **younger sibling** (brother or sister)

phîi-nóng พี่น้อง **brothers and sisters** (collectively)

Other terms:

phîi săaw พี่สาว **older sister**
phîi chaay พี่ชาย **older brother**
náwng săow น้องสาว **younger sister**
náwng chaay น้องชาย **younger brother**

phîi khěui พี่เขย
brother-in-law (husband of older sister)

nóng khěui น้องเขย
brother-in-law (husband of younger sister)

phîi saphái พี่สะใภ้
sister-in-law (wife of older brother)

nóng saphái น้องสะใภ้
sister-in-law (wife of younger brother)

phîi líang พี่เลี้ยง **nurse (maid)**

Cultural note

Thai society seems to take more interest in the relations between people than a Western one does. This applies in particular to the relationships within the family, but the idea of "family" is extended beyond one's own real, blood, relatives to include others one comes into contact with. This is why people who are actually not related can address each other as *phîi* พี่ (elder brother/sister) or *nóng* น้อง (younger brother/sister), depending on their age. In this way everybody gets fitted into a framework of status and, consequently, of mutual obligations. In the "family" hierarchy, the younger members have to listen to and accept the judgments of the older ones. This can have benefits in terms of assistance and protection, but it also involves a degree of frustration and resentment in the face of tyranny from above.

So age difference is built into the terms for siblings, but not gender—the same terms apply to male and female siblings.

For more kinship terms, refer to page 135.

For more kinship terms, refer to page 135.

54

MIA เมีย **wife** (informal); PHAN-RÁ-YAA ภรรยา **wife** (formal)

Phǒm phaa phan-rá-yaa bpai hǎa mǒr.
ผมพาภรรยาไปหาหมอ
I took my wife to see a doctor.

Mia thórng เมียท้อง **She is pregnant.**

mia nói เมียน้อย
a junior wife (unofficial, second wife; mistress)

55

PHǓA ผัว **husband** (informal, impolite); SǍAMII สามี **husband** (formal)

Sǎamii khǒng chǎn bpen khon dii.
สามีของฉันเป็นคนดี
My husband is a good person.

Sǎamii tham ngaan nàk. สามีทำงานหนัก
My husband works hard.

Phǔa khîi-mao, mâi dii. ผัวขี้เมาไม่ดี
A drunkard husband is not good.

PHÊUAN เพื่อน friend, companion

Rau bpen phêuan gan. เราเป็นเพื่อนกัน
We are friends.

Rau rák phêuan. เรารักเพื่อน
We love our friends.

Khău mii phêuan mâak. เขามีเพื่อนมาก
He/she has many friends.

Terms:

phêuan khûu-jai เพื่อนคู่ใจ **a trusted friend**
phêuan bâan เพื่อนบ้าน **a neighbor**
phêuan chaai เพื่อนชาย **a male friend**
phêuan yĭng เพื่อนหญิง **a female friend**

BUT

faen แฟน **girlfriend/boyfriend** (from English "fan," admirer!)

Cultural note

Going to visit a friend

When visiting a friend, don't forget that you will have to take off your shoes before entering the house or apartment. This rule applies to anyone's home, but not a public building, unless a sign tells you otherwise: ***garunaa thòrt rohng-tháau*** กรุณาถอดรองเท้า, "kindly remove your shoes."

Thai people enjoy sitting around on the floor (on mats), even to enjoy a meal. In this case, be careful not to point your feet at other people, as this is considered extremely rude.

You should not stand over someone else's head, and if you have to pass something over their shoulder, say ***Khòr thôot*** ขอโทษ, "Excuse me."

It is not necessary to bring a present, but a contribution to the food or drink would of course be appreciated.

57 BÂANG บ้าง else (in conjunction with a question word)

NOTE: It is placed after a question word when more than one answer to the question is possible.

Krâwp-krua khǎwng khun mii krai bâang?
ครอบครัวของคุณมีใครบ้าง
Who are they in your family?

→ ***Mii phâw, mâe, phîi-chaay, náwng-sǎow kàp phǒm.***
มีพ่อ แม่ พี่ชาย น้องสาว กับ ผม
They are my father, mother, elder brother, younger sister, and me.

Khun mii phêuan chûe àrai bâang?
คุณมีเพื่อนชื่ออะไรบ้าง
What are the names of your Thai friends?

→ *Mii chûe Nid, Kai, Taai, kàp Joy.*
มีชื่อ นิด ไก่ ต่าย กับ จอย
They are Nid, Kai, Taai, and Joy.

Khun chôrp bpai-thîaw thîi-nǎi bâang?
คุณชอบไปเที่ยวที่ไหนบ้าง
Where (else) do you like to visit?

→ *Chǎn chôrp bpai-thîaw Chiang Mai, Phuket, kàp Krabi.*
ฉันชอบไปเที่ยวเชียงใหม่ ภูเก็ต กับ กระบี่
I'd like to go to Chiang Mai, Phuket, and Krabi.

58 RŬE หรือ or

Khun mii phîi săaw rŭe phîi-chaay?
คุณมีพี่สาวหรือพี่ชาย
Do you have an older sister or older brother?

Khun chôrp aa-hăan Thai rŭe aa-hăan Amerigan?
คุณชอบอาหารไทยหรืออาหารอเมริกัน
Do you like Thai food or American food?

59 DTÀENG-NGAAN แต่งงาน
to get married

Khun dtàeng-ngaan rĕu yang? คุณแต่งงานหรือยัง
Are you married (or not yet)?

→ *Dtàeng-ngaan láew.* แต่งงานแล้ว **I'm married.**

→ *Bpen sòht.* เป็นโสด
I am unmarried (live a single life).

→ *Yâek-gan yùu.* แยกกันอยู่
I am separated (from my husband/wife).

→ *Yàa láew.* หย่าแล้ว **I am divorced.**

→ *Bpen mâe-mâai.* เป็นแม่หม้าย **I am a widow.**

→ *Bpen phôr-mâai.* เป็นพ่อหม้าย
I am a widower.

JAI ใจ **heart, mind**

Phôr bpen khon yang-ngai? เขาเป็นคนยังไง
What sort of person is he/she?

→ *Phôr (bpen khon) jai-dii.* พ่อ (เป็นคน) ใจดี
   **My father is a kindhearted (good-natured)
   person.**

jai-yen ใจเย็น **calm, cool-headed**

jai-rórn ใจร้อน **impatient**

jai-dam ใจดำ **mean, selfish**

jai-ráai ใจร้าย **to be cruel, mean**

jai-gwâang ใจกว้าง **to be generous, open-minded**

jai-khâep ใจแคบ **to be narrow-minded**

There are many interesting expressions containing the
word *jai* ใจ, some useful for understanding Thai values.
Here is a selection (there are nouns, verbs and adjectives):

grengjai เกรงใจ **consideration; to be reluctant to
impose on others**

jing-jai จริงใจ **sincere, heartfelt**

Khòrp-jai! ขอบใจ **Thanks!** (informal)

khâu-jai เข้าใจ **to understand**

bplìan jai เปลี่ยนใจ **to change one's mind**

jèp-jai เจ็บใจ **hurt, offended**

jai-ngâai ใจง่าย **easy to get (woman)**

jai-dtên ใจเต้น **excited, with pounding heart**

jai-loy ใจลอย **to be absent-minded / zone out**

jai-sĭa ใจเสีย **disheartened; to lose heart**

cheun-jai ชื่นใจ **pleased, delighted, elated**

nám-jai น้ำใจ **thoughtfulness, goodwill**

sŏn-jai สนใจ **interested, absorbed (in)**

wăan-jai หวานใจ **sweetheart**

hŭa-jai หัวใจ **the heart** (anatomical)

Entertainments

61 **THÎAU** เที่ยว **trip, excursion, traveling about**

bpai thîau ไปเที่ยว **to go around (for pleasure),
to go out (e.g. for the evening)**

thîi thîau ที่เที่ยว **a place to go, to tour around**

maa thîau มาเที่ยว **to come around (to someone's
house, for a visit)**

bpai thîau glaang kheun ไปเที่ยวกลางคืน
to go out late at night

Bpai thîau gan theu'… . ไปเที่ยวกันเถอะ
Let's go out together.

62 **DUU** ดู **to watch, look at**

duu thiiwii thîi bâan ดูทีวีที่บ้าน
to watch TV at home

bpai duu năng ไปดูหนัง
to go and see a movie/film

NOTE: the Thai word *fiim* ฟีม refers only to photographic
film.

duu show ดูโชว์ to watch a show

Mii show lăai yàang. มีโชว์หลายอย่าง
There are shows of many kinds.

Mii show dtorn dtèuk. มีโชว์ตอนดึก
There are late-night shows.

duu lakhorn ดูละคร to watch a play/drama

duu gilaa ดูกีฬา to watch sport/a game

khâa duu ค่าดู admission fee

63   LÊN เล่น to play; to do something for fun/ amusement, not seriously

deun lên เดินเล่น to go for a stroll

gin lên กินเล่น to have a snack

phûut lên พูดเล่น to joke around, tease

norn lên นอนเล่น to have a snooze

lên gilaa เล่นกีฬา to play sport/a game

lên fútbon เล่นฟุตบอล to play football (that is, soccer, not other kinds)

lên dondtrii เล่นดนตรี to play music

lên gii-dtâa เล่นกีต้าร์ to play the guitar

DTÊN เต้น to dance;
RAM รำ Thai traditional dance

ram Thai รำไทย classical Thai dance

ram wong รำวง folk dance (couples moving in
a circle)

ram séung รำเซิ้ง
name of a folk dance from the North-East

Mii dtên ago-go thîi night-club.
มีเต้นอโกโก้ที่ไน้ท์คลับ
There is ago-go dancing in the night club.

Phŏm chôrp dtên. ผมชอบเต้น **I like dancing.**

Phŏm dtên/ram mâi bpen.
ผม เต้น/รำ ไม่เป็น
I can't dance/perform Thai traditional dance.

(Note that *bpen* here means "to be able," in the sense of
having a particular skill.)

Khun dtên/ram gàp phŏm mái?
คุณเต้น/รำ กับผมไหม
Will you dance/perform the Thai dance with me?

65 | PLEHNG เพลง song/music

rórng plehng ร้องเพลง to sing a song

fang plehng ฟังเพลง to listen to music

dtàeng plehng แต่งเพลง to compose a song

nák dtàeng plehng นักแต่งเพลง a song writer, composer

thamnorng plehng ทำนองเพลง melody, tune

néua plehng เนื้อเพลง lyrics

plehng châat เพลงชาติ the national anthem

plehng Thai deum เพลงไทยเดิม classical Thai music

plehng Thai saagon เพลงไทยสากล modern Thai music

plehng faràng เพลงฝรั่ง Western music

plehng pheun-bâan เพลงพื้นบ้าน regional music

66 | SÀNÙK สนุก to have fun, enjoy oneself; to be fun, amusing, entertaining

Bpai thîau Chiang Mai sànùk.
ไปเที่ยวเชียงใหม่สนุก
I enjoyed my trip in Chiang Mai.

Rórng plehng sànùk mâak. ร้องเพลงสนุกมาก
I had so much fun with singing.

nâa-sanùk น่าสนุก **to be fun, enjoyable**

sanùk dii สนุกดี **to be good fun; to have a good time**

67 NÂA น่า

It is attached to verbs with the meaning of "inviting," "inducing," "to be worth doing."

Ráan-aa-hăan ráan níi nâa gin. อาหารร้านนี้น่ากิน
The food at this restaurant looks delicious.

Chiang Mai nâa thîaw. เชียงใหม่น่าเที่ยว
Chiang Mai is worth visiting.

Năng rêuang níi nâa duu. หนังเรื่องนี้น่าดู
This movie is worth watching.

Năng-sĕu lêm níi nâa àan. หนังสือเล่มนี้น่าอ่าน
This book is worth reading.

Plehng Thai nâa sŏn-jai. เพลงไทยน่าสนใจ
Thai music is interesting.

68 PEN เป็น **to know how/to have ability;**
MÂI PEN ไม่เป็น **unable to do something**

Chăn lên gii-tâa pen tàe lên pia-no mâi pen.
ฉันเล่นกีตาร์เป็น แต่เล่นเปียโนไม่เป็น
I know how to play the guitar but not the piano.

Chăn wâay-náam pen tàe khìi jàk-gà-yaan mâi pen.
ฉันว่ายน้ำเป็น แต่ขี่จักรยานไม่เป็น
I know how to swim but not ride a bike.

Khun lên football pen mái? คุณเล่นฟุตบอลเป็นไหม
Do you know how to play football?

NOTE: In addition to talk about capability/ability, you can use *dâi* ได้/*mâi dâi* ไม่ได้ (to be able to/not able to). It has a broader meaning than *pen*/*mâi pen* because it's not only you don't know how to do something, but you also are not physically able to do it.

69 GWÀA กว่า is used to make comparison; MÂAK GWÀA มากกว่า more than

NOTE: The comparative is formed by putting *gwàa* กว่า after the adjective or adverb.

    subject + adjective/adverb + *gwàa* + subject

Krung-thep rórn gwàa Chiang Mai.
กรุงเทพร้อนกว่าเชียงใหม่
Bangkok is hotter than Chiang Mai.

Chăn chôrp aa-hăan thai mâak gwàa aa-hăan jiin.
ฉันชอบอาหารไทยมากกว่าอาหารจีน
I like Thai food more than Chinese food.

Phǒm chôrp dtên mâak gwàa rórng-plehng.
ผมชอบเต้นมากกว่าร้องเพลง
I like singing more than dancing.

70 THÌ-SÙT ที่สุด extremely, the most

NOTE: The superlative is formed by putting *thîi sùt* ที่สุด
after the adjective or adverb.

subject + adjective/adverb + *thîi sùt*

Chǎn chôrp duu nǎng mâak thîi sùt.
ฉันชอบดูหนังมากที่สุด
I like watching movies the most.

Mâe khǒrng phǒm jai dii thîi sùt. แม่ของผมใจดีที่สุด
My mother is extremely kind. (lit. "My mother is
the kindest.")

Thá-le thîi Phuket sǔai thîi sùt. ทะเลที่ภูเก็ตสวยที่สุด
The beach in Phuket is the most beautiful.

Aa-hǎan Thai phèt thîi sùt. อาหารไทยเผ็ดที่สุด
Thai food is extremely spicy.

Telling and talking

71 **WÂA** ว่า **that**

Grammatical note

This word comes after verbs used for reporting what someone has said. It can be translated with "that" or "whether" (asking), or nothing, where it introduces a clause. For examples, see the following.

72 **BÒRK** บอก **to say, tell, inform**

Khun Tony bòrk wâa, khău chôrp bia Cháang.
คุณโทนี่บอกว่าเขาชอบเบียร์ช้าง
Tony said that he likes Elephant beer.

Khău bòrk wâa, mii mia láew.
เขาบอกว่ามีเมียแล้ว
He said he already had a wife.

Chăn bòrk Mali wâa, yàa gèp ngeun thîi bon dtók.
ฉันบอกมะลิว่าอย่าเก็บเงินที่บนโต๊ะ
I told Mali not to (don't) take the money on the table.

Bòrk mâi thùuk. บอกไม่ถูก
It's hard to say exactly.

73 PHÛUT พูด to speak, talk, say

Phûut phaasăa Anggrìt dâi mái?
พูดภาษาอังกฤษได้ไหม
Can you speak English?

→ *Phûut dâi nít nòi.* พูดได้นิดหน่อย
I can speak it a bit.

Note the word order with *dâi* ได้ here.

→ *Phûut cháa-cháa nòi, (khráp/kà).*
พูดช้าๆหน่อย (ครับ/ค่ะ)
Please speak slowly.

Khău phûut gèng. เขาพูดเก่ง
He/she's good at speaking (it).

NOTE: The word *gèng* เก่ง, "skilled, good at something," is placed after the verb it refers to.

Chau bâan phûut. ชาวบ้านพูด
The villagers are talking (gossiping).

74 THĂAM ถาม to ask (a question)

Khun Nók thăam wâa rau jà' maa mêua-rài.
คุณนกถามว่าเราจะมาเมื่อไร
Nok asked when we would come.

Thǎam wâa… ถามว่า **May I ask…**

Jerry thǎam wâa rau mii wehlaa réu bplàu.
เจอรี่ถามว่าเรามีเวลาหรือเปล่า
Jerry asked whether (if) we have time or not.

NOTE: "if" in a conditional sense is *thâa* ถ้า, e.g. *Thâa yàang nán…* ถ้าอย่างนั้น "If that's the case/in that case…"

75 BPLAE แปล to mean (by explanation, translation); to translate

bplae wâa… แปลว่า **that means, that is to say…**

Nîi bplae wâa à-rai? นี่แปลว่าอะไร
What does this mean?

Chûay bplae jòtmǎi jàak faen.
ช่วยแปลจดหมายจากแฟน
Please help translate this letter from my girlfriend.

76 RÎAK เรียก to be called; to call

Khǒng nîi rîak wâa à-rai?
ของนี้เรียกว่าอะไร
What's this thing called?

Phonlamái níi rîak wâa mangkhút.
ผลไม้นี้เรียกว่ามังคุด
This fruit is called a mangosteen.

Rîak dtamrùat! เรียกตำรวจ **Call the police!**

77 KHÍT คิด to think, reckon, calculate

Khău khít wâa khon Thai jai dii mâak.
เขาคิดว่าคนไทยใจดีมาก
He thinks Thai people are very kind.

khwaam khít ความคิด **thought**

khít lêhk คิดเลข **to do sums** (literally, "reckon figures")

Khít ngeun dûai. คิดเงินด้วย **Check the bill, please.**

Khít mâi òrk. คิดไม่ออก **I can't figure it out.**

khít thěung คิดถึง **thinking of you (missing you)** (at end of a letter).

lorng khít duu ลองคิดดู **to think something over**

NOTE: The word *lorng* ลอง means "to try out," so here, to try and see what something is like by thinking it over.

78   RÚU   รู้   to know

Chăn rúu wâa khăo chôrp gin aa-hăan Thai.
ฉันรู้ว่าเขาชอบกินอาหารไทย
I know that he likes to eat Thai food.

Khun rúu mái wâa ráan gaa-fae pòet gìi-mong?
คุณรู้ไหมว่าร้านกาแฟเปิดกี่โมง
Do you know what time the coffee shop is open?

Phŏm mâi rúu wâa rong-raem yùu thîi-năi.
ผมไม่รู้ว่าโรงแรมอยู่ที่ไหน
I don't know where the hotel is.

79   WĂNG   หวัง   to hope

Chăn wăng wâa jà pai sà-năam-bin than we-laa.
ฉันหวังว่าจะไปสนามบินทันเวลา
I hope to get to the airport in time.

Prûng-níi wăng wâa fŏn jà mâi tòk.
พรุ่งนี้หวังว่าฝนจะไม่ตก
I hope that it won't be raining tomorrow.

khwaam wăng ความหวัง hope

khít wăng ผิดหวัง to be disappointed

RÚU-SÙEK รู้สึก to feel

Chăn rúu-sùek wâa khăo mâi chôrp chăn.
ฉันรู้สึกว่าเขาไม่ชอบฉัน
I feel he doesn't like me.

Phŏm rúu-sùek wâa wan níi rórn mâak.
ผมรู้สึกว่าวันนี้ร้อนมาก
I feel that today is very hot.

Grammatical note

Rúu-sùek (รู้สึก) can be used to talk about or express your feelings.

Bpen yàng-ngai bâang? เป็นยังไงบ้าง
How are you?

→ *Rúu-sùek <u>nùeay</u>.* รู้สึกเหนื่อย **I feel <u>tired</u>.**

Substitute the noun underlined:

mâi sà-baai ไม่สบาย **not feeling well/to be sick**

ngûang-nawn ง่วงนอน **sleepy**

bùea เบื่อ **bored**

aay อาย **shy**

glua กลัว **scared**

bùea เบื่อ

gròt โกรธ

glua กลัว

tùen-tên ตื่นเต้น

sǐa-jai เสียใจ **sad**

gròt โกรธ **angry**

dii-jai ดีใจ **happy**

rórn ร้อน **hot**

tùen-tên ตื่นเต้น **excited**

nǎow หนาว **cold**

Health and the body

81   **BPÙAT** ปวด **to ache**

bpùat hŭa ปวดหัว **(to have a) headache**

thórng ปวดท้อง **stomach-ache**

fan ปวดฟัน **toothache**

hŭu ปวดหู **earache**

lăng ปวดหลัง **backache**

khăa ขา **leg pain**

82   **JÈP** เจ็บ **to hurt, be sore**

Jèp dtrong nĭi? เจ็บตรงไหน **Where does it hurt?**

→ *Jèp dtrong nĭi.* เจ็บตรงนี้ **It hurts here** (pointing).

jèp khor เจ็บคอ **to have a sore throat**

jèp-taa เจ็บตา **sore eyes**

83   **BPEN** เป็น **to suffer** (from an illness)

bpen wàt เป็นหวัด **to have a cold**

Khau bpen wàt. เขาเป็นหวัด **He has a <u>cold</u>.**

Substitute the noun underlined:

bpen khâi ไข้ **to have a fever (temperature)**

bpen khâi wàt ไข้หวัด **to have the flu**

bpen phlăe แผล **to have a wound (cut, sore place)**

bpen lom เป็นลม **to feel faint**

bpen rôhk AIDS โรคเอดส์ (pron. "ehd") **to have AIDS**

bpen gaam-má-rôhk กามโรค **to suffer from an STD**

bpen maigren ไมเกรน **to have a migraine headache**

bpen hòrp-hèut หอบหืด **to have asthma**

84   PHÁE แพ้   to be allergic to

Chăn pháe aa-hăan thá-le. ฉันแพ้อาหารทะเล
I'm allergic to seafood.

pháe thùa แพ้ถั่ว **peanut allergy**

pháe yaa แพ้ยา **drug allergy**

pháe aa-gàat แพ้อากาศ **hay fever**

pháe fùn แพ้ฝุ่น **dust allergy**

pháe khŏn maew/măa แพ้ขนแมว/หมา
cat/dog allergies

yaa gâe pháe ยาแก้แพ้ **antihistamine**

85 AAGAAN อาการ symptom(s)

Aagaan bpen yaang-rai? อาการเป็นอย่างไร
What are the symptoms?

→ **Aagaan mâi dii.** อาการ ไม่ ดี
   The symptoms don't look good.

aajian อาเจียน **vomiting** (informal: *ûak* อ้วก)
bpen khâi sŭung เป็นไข้สูง **high fever**
wian-hŭa เวียนหัว **dizziness**
norn mâi láp นอนไม่หลับ **can't sleep**

Gin ahăan mâi dâi. กินอาหารไม่ได้
I can't eat. No appetite.

ai ไอ **coughing**
thórng deun ท้องเดิน **to have a "running stomach"**
thórng sĭa ท้องเสีย **to have an upset stomach**
thórng rûang ท้องร่วง **to have diarrhea**
nám mûuk lăi น้ำมูกไหล **to have a runny nose**

86 YAA ยา medicine; drugs

chìit yaa ฉีดยา **to inject a drug or medicine**
yaa mét ยาเม็ด **tablet, pill**
yaa náam ยาน้ำ **liquid medicine**

yaa gâe ai ยาแก้ไอ cough medicine

yaa yòrt dtaa ยาหยอดตา eye drops

bai sàng yaa ใบสั่งยา prescription

yaa thàay ยาถ่าย laxative

yaa bâa ยาบ้า amphetamines

yaa sùup ยาสูบ tobacco

mau yaa เมายา drugged, doped

87 HĂAI หาย to get well

Hăai láew. หายแล้ว
I'm better (the illness has gone).

Hăai bpùai réu yang? หายป่วยหรือยัง
Have you recovered from your sickness yet?

Hăai jèp mái? หายเจ็บไหม
Have you got over the soreness?

88 DTÔRNG ต้อง have to, must

Khun pen wàt dtôrng gin ya. คุณเป็นหวัด ต้องกินยา
You have a cold, so you have to take some medicine.

Dtôrng phák phòrn. ต้องพักผ่อน
You have to get some rest.

Dtôrng pai hăa mŏr. ต้องไปหาหมอ
You have to see the doctor.

Dtôrng pai rong-phá-yaa-baan. ต้องไปโรงพยาบาล
You must go to the hospital.

89 THÙUK ถูก

is used in passive sentences when referring to events of violent or unpleasant nature. For example:

thùuk dtii ถูกตี **to be hit**

thùuk dtòy ถูกต่อย **to be punched**

thùuk jàp ถูกจับ **to be arrested**

thùuk khà-moi ถูกขโมย **to be stolen**

Khăo thùuk rót chon เขาถูกรถชน
He got hit by a car

Dèk thùuk măa gàt เด็กถูกหมากัด
A child is bitten by a dog

90 KHÛEN ขึ้น

is used to imply that something gets improved. For example:

dii khûen ดีขึ้น **better**

113

sǔay khûen สวยขึ้น **more beautiful**

sǔung khûen สูงขึ้น **taller**

gèng khûen เก่งขึ้น **more skillful**

Mêua waan níi pùat hǔa tàe dii khûen láew.
เมื่อวานนี้ปวดหัว แต่ดีขึ้นแล้ว
Yesterday I had a headache, but I feel better now.

Thâa aa-gaan mâi dii khûen khun dtôrng pai hǎa mǒr.
ถ้าอาการไม่ดีขึ้น คุณต้องไปหาหมอ
If the conditions haven't improved, you must see the doctor.

Cultural notes

Body parts

In Thai culture, different body parts are worthy of different levels of respect. Remember that Thais place special emphasis on three main body parts: the head, the hands, and the feet. Thais dislike being touched anywhere.

Head: The head is considered the most respected and the most important part of the entire body. You should never touch anyone's head for any reason.

Hands: Don't point with the forefinger at anyone. Also, it is more acceptable and polite to use the right hand when giving and receiving things, and putting things into the mouth. This is because the left hand is used to clean oneself after going to the toilet.

Feet: The feet are considered the dirtiest part of the body because they are in contact with the ground. Therefore, don't point your feet (with or without shoes on) towards a person, or religious image or a picture of the Royal Family. Also, don't use your feet to move anything or touch anyone. Lastly, you should not step over any part of the body of a person that is lying down.

Traveling/Banking/Using phones and Internet

91 **RÓT** รถ **vehicle/transport** (lit: "car")

Mii rót-fai pai Chiang Mai gìi-mong?
มีรถไฟไปเชียงใหม่กี่โมง
When is there a train to Chiang Mai?

Rót-fai àwk gìi-mong? รถไฟออกกี่โมง
What time does the train leave?

Rót-fai thǔeng gìi-mong? รถไฟถึงกี่โมง
What time does the train arrive?

Khûen rót thîi chaan-chaa-laa nǎi?
ขึ้นรถที่ชานชาลาไหน
Which platform/terminal can I get on the transport?

rót-may รถเมล์ **non air-con bus/metro bus**

rót-thua รถทัวร์ **air-con bus/coach**

pâay-rót-may ป้ายรถเมล์ **bus stop**

rót-fai-fáa รถไฟฟ้า **skytrain (BTS)**

rót-fai-tâi-din รถไฟใต้ดิน **subway (MRT)**

rót-sŏng-thăew รถสองแถว **two-row minibus**

rót-fai รถไฟ **train**

rót-tham-má-daa รถธรรมดา **ordinary train**

rót-rew รถเร็ว **rapid train**

rót-dùan รถด่วน **express train**

rót-dùan-phí-sèt รถด่วนพิเศษ **special express train**

khâa-rót ค่ารถ **fare**

rót-gĕng รถเก๋ง **car**

rót-dtôu รถตู้ **van**

92 DTŬA ตั๋ว ticket

Khăw jawng dtŭa pai Pattaya săwng thîi-nâng.
ขอจองตั๋วไปพัทยาสองที่นั่ง
I'd like to reserve two seats to Pattaya.

Khâa-dtŭa thîaw-diaw thâo-rài?
ค่าตั๋วเที่ยวเดียวเท่าไร
How much is a one-way ticket?

Khâa-dtŭa pai-klàp thâo-rài? ค่าตั๋วไปกลับเท่าไร
How much is a round trip ticket?

khâa-dtŭa ค่าตั๋ว **fare**

hâwng-khăay-dtŭa ห้องขายตั๋ว **ticket office**

thîaw-diaw เที่ยวเดียว **single (ticket)**

pai-klàp ไปกลับ **return (ticket)**

hâwng-khǎay-dtǔa ห้องขายตั๋ว **ticket office**

93 HÀANG ห่าง to be far away (distance)

Chiang Mai yùu hàang jàak Krungthep gìi gìloh?
เชียงใหม่อยู่ห่างจากกรุงเทพกี่กิโล
How far away (lit: how many kilometers) **is Chiang Mai from Bangkok?**

Rong-raem yùu hàang jàak sà-nǎam-bin prà-maan yîi sìp naa-thii.
โรงแรมอยู่ห่างจากสนามบินประมาณ 20 นาที
The hotel is about 20 minutes away from the airport.

94 PHÁK พัก to stay

Pai-thîaw Phuket khun phák thîi-nǎi?
ไปเที่ยวภูเก็ต คุณพักที่ไหน
Where will you be staying in Phuket?

Phǒm khít wâa jà phák rong-raem.
ผมคิดว่าจะพักโรงแรม
I think I will stay in a hotel.

hǒr phák หอพัก **dorm**

phák phòrn พักผ่อน **to rest**

phák rórn พักร้อน **vacation**

NOTE: *phák* พัก also means "to take a break." For example:

Phák hâa naa thii. พัก 5 นาที
Let's take 5-minutes break.

95 HÔRNG ห้อง room

Mii hôrng wâang mái? มีห้องว่างไหม
Are there any rooms available?

Jorng hôrng dâi mái? จองห้องได้ไหม
May I reserve a room?

Hôrng dtiang dìaw rǔe dtiang khûu?
ห้องเตียงเดี่ยวหรือเตียงคู่
Do you want a single room or double room?

Khǒr plìan hôrng dâi mái? ขอเปลี่ยนห้องได้ไหม
May I change rooms?

Khǒr duu hôrng dâi mái? ขอดูห้องได้ไหม
May I see the room first?

hôrng nám ห้องน้ำ **bathroom**

hôrng norn ห้องนอน **bedroom**

hôrng khrua ห้องครัว **kitchen**

hôrng ae ห้องแอร์ **air-conditioned room**

hôrng tham-má-daa ห้องธรรมดา **regular room**

96 NGEUN เงิน money

Khŏr lâek dollar bpen ngeun bàht?
ขอแลกดอลลาร์เป็นเงินบาท
May I exchange dollars for baht?

(Note the use of *bpen* เป็น "be, become" here.)

Khŏr lâek-ngoen nùeng-rói dawn-lâa.
ขอแลกเงิน 100 ดอลล่าร์
I'd like to exchange 100 USD.

Khŏr thŏrn-ngeun săwng-phan bàat.
ขอถอนเงิน 2,000 บาท
I'd like to deposit 2000 baht.

Khŏr bank hâa róoi bàht sŏrng bai?
ขอแบงค์ห้าร้อยบาทสองใบ
May I have two banknotes of 500 baht?

lâek-ngeun แลกเงิน **exchange money**

thŏrn-ngeun ถอนเงิน **withdraw (money)**

fàak-ngeun ฝากเงิน **deposit (money)**

on-ngeun โอนเงิน **transfer money**

lâek chék แลกเช็ค **exchange a (traveler's) check**

Useful phrases relating to money:

Khŏr ngeun thorn. ขอเงินทอน
May I have my change?

Ngeun thorn thâu-rài? เงินทอนเท่าไร
How much is the change?

Mâi dtông thorn. ไม่ต้องทอน
No need to give change (keep the change).

Phŏm hâi thíp khun. ผมให้ทิปคุณ
It's a tip for you.

NOTES

1. The Thai for "banknote" is just *bank* แบ็งค์. The counting word for banknotes is *bai* ใบ "leaf."

2. There is a different word for "change" (money given back after a transaction), namely *ngeun thorn* เงิน ทอน (pronounced "torn").

97 Thoh โทร to make a call

thoh-rá-sàp โทรศัพท์ **phone**
boe (thoh-rá-sàp) เบอร์ (โทรศัพท์) **phone number**
meu-thěu มือถือ **mobile phone**
thoh-hǎa โทรหา **give someone a call**

thoh-maa โทรมา **someone called you**

hâi-thoh-klàp ให้โทรกลับ **return a call, call back**

Khǎw boe (thoh-rá-sàp) dâi-mái?
ขอเบอร์ (โทรศัพท์) ได้ไหม
Could I get your phone number, please?

Khun mii boe meu-thěu Khun Somsak mái?
คุณมีเบอร์มือถือคุณสมศักดิ์ไหม
Do you have Mr. Somsak's mobile phone number?

98 CHÛAY ช่วย Could you please?/Please

NOTE: It is usually placed in the beginning of a sentence in order to soften a request or ask for a favor or assistance.

Chûay bòrk khǎo wâa phǒm thoh-maa.
ช่วยบอกเขาว่าผมโทรมา
Please tell him that I called.

Chûay bòrk khǎo hâi-thoh-klàp boe sǒun-pàet-kâo-jèt-sǎam-sǎam-hâa-pàet-jèt-sìi.
ช่วยบอกเขาให้โทรกลับเบอร์ 089-7335874
Please tell him/her to call me back at 089-7335874.

Chûay bàwk khǎo thoh-hǎa chǎn boe sǒun-sìi-
sǎam-sǎam-sìi-sǎwng-kâo-nùeng-sǎam.
ช่วยบอกเขาโทรหาฉัน เบอร์ 043-342913
Please tell her to give me a call at 043-342913.

99 SĂAY สาย line (telephone connection)

phôut พูด speak

ráp-sǎay รับสาย answer/pick up the phone

waang-sǎay วางสาย hang up the phone

fàk-khâw-khwaam ฝากข้อความ leave a message

mâi-yòu ไม่อยู่ **(person) is not in.**

Sǎay-mâi-wâang. สายไม่ว่าง **The line is busy/engaged.**

Han-lǒ khǎw phôut kàp Khun Somjai?
ฮัลโหล ขอพูดกับคุณสมใจ
Hello. May I speak to Ms. Somjai, please?

→ *Kam-lang phôut.* กำลังพูด
  I'm speaking./Speaking.

→ *Raw-sàk-krôu.* รอสักครู่
  Hold the line, please.

→ *Khun Somjai mâi-yòu.* คุณสมใจไม่อยู่
  Ms. Somjai is not in.

→ *Khun Somjai mâi-wâang ráp-sǎay.*
  คุณสมใจไม่ว่างรับสาย
  Ms. Somjai is too busy (to answer the phone).

124

→ *Săay-mâi-wâang.* สายไม่ว่าง
The line is busy at the moment.

IN-TOE-NÈT อินเตอร์เน็ต **Internet**

waay-faay วายฟาย **Wi-Fi connection**

ii-meo อีเมล์ **email address**

tàw ต่อ **connect**

khâo เข้า **get access**

rá-hàt รหัส **password**

sòng ส่ง **send**

Chăn khâo in-toe-nèt mâi-dâi.
ฉันเข้าอินเตอร์เน็ตไม่ได้
I cannot get access to the Internet.

Khun mii waay-faay mái? คุณมีวายฟายไหม
Do you have a Wi-Fi connection?

125

Khăw rá-hàt waay-faay dâi-mái?

ขอรหัสวายฟายได้ไหม

Could I get a Wi-Fi password, please?

Chăn/phŏm tàw waay-faay mâi-dâi.

ฉัน/ผม ต่อวายฟายไม่ได้

I cannot connect to the Wi-Fi.

Chăn/phŏm sòng ii-meo mâi-dâi.

ฉัน/ผม ส่งอีเมล์ไม่ได้   **I cannot send my email.**

Cultural notes

Cell phone

- It is very easy and cheap to buy a local (basic) cell phone with a Thai SIM card at any phone shop in any shopping mall. If you have your own cell phone, you can just go to any 7-11 stores or other convenience stores to buy a Thai SIM card. You can also get top-up cards of 50, 100, 200, and 300 baht. These credits can be used for calling and sending text messages (including International calls, but read the dialing instructions carefully). You can also apply your credit to an "Internet Package" which allows you browsing throughout Thailand.

- If you want to use your own phone, bear in mind that most cell phones from the U.S. are locked and cannot be used on other networks. If you want to use a U.S.

phone with a Thai SIM card, you need to make sure that it is unlocked. Most European cell phones will work in Thailand without any hassle. However, you are advised to check with your mobile service provider before your departure to avoid any unpleasant surprises.

Internet access

Internet is readily available in major cities in Thailand, but still not that common in remote rural areas. Many hotels offer in-room wireless services free of charge. You will probably be able to get free Wi-Fi in countless cafés, restaurants, and hotel lobbies as well. You can also find a lot of cybercafés or Internet cafes, especially in the tourist areas. They offer cheap Internet access at hourly rates, and usually serve snacks and drinks as well.

Appendices

Top Tourist Destinations and Shopping

Thailand is filled with spectacular natural, cultural, historical attractions, and is a great place for shopping as you can find lots of mega shopping malls, local markets, night markets, department stores, and independent boutiques.

The Grand Palace (พระบรมมหาราชวัง *Phra Borom Maha Ratcha Wang*)—It is the most famous landmark in Bangkok. The Grand Palace is built in 1782 (during the reign of King Rama I) to become a royal residence, and it has been the utmost architectural symbol of Thailand ever since. It served as a significant royal residence until 1925 and is now used for ceremonial purposes only.

The Temple of the Emerald Buddha (วัดพระแก้ว *Wat Phra Kaew*)—It is regarded as the most important Buddhist temple in Thailand and located in the historic center of Bangkok, within the grounds of the Grand Palace. The Emerald Buddha in the temple is deeply revered and venerated in Thailand as the protector of the country.

Wat Arun (วัดอรุณ)—It is situated on the west bank of the Chao Phraya River and is also known as the Temple of the Dawn. It has an imposing spire over 70 meters high, beautifully decorated with tiny pieces of colored glass and Chinese porcelain placed delicately into intricate patterns.

Khao San Road (ถนนข้าวสาร)—"Khao San" translates as "milled rice." It has everything a backpacker would need: a wide range of budget accommodations, an array of restaurants and bars, Thai street dishes, money exchange counters, and tour operators. You can also find handcrafts, paintings, clothes, and second-hand books.

Chatuchak Weekend Market (ตลาดจตุจักร)—It is one of the world's largest weekend markets in Bangkok and covers an area of 27 acres. The market offers a wide variety of products including household items, clothing, Thai handicrafts, religious artifacts, collectables, foods, and live animals.

Pratunam (ประตูน้ำ)—It is Thailand's largest clothing market. You'll find all sorts of fashion apparels at best bargained prices for wholesales. This may be the cheapest market for buying clothes, fabrics and textiles in central Bangkok.

Asiatique the Riverfront (เอเชียทีค)—Asiatique has successfully combined two of the most popular shopping experiences in the city: a night bazaar and a mall. With over 1,500 boutiques and 40 restaurants housed under a huge replica warehouse complex, you'll have good fun browsing the boutiques, picking up gifts, and eating good food.

Shopping Malls in Bangkok

Bangkok has more than enough shopping malls to suit all kinds of lifestyles and budgets. You will find from the legendary **MBK**, to the sophisticated **Emporium**, **Siam Discovery**,

Central World Plaza, **Siam Paragon**, **Terminal 21**, and the latest ultra-luxury **Central Embassy**. In these malls you can find fine-dining restaurants, the city's finest fashion stores, global brands, bookshops, specialty stores, accessories stands and all kinds of luxury designer stores.

Amphawa Floating Market (ตลาดน้ำอัมพวา *Ta Laad Nam Amphawa*)—It is located 50 km from Bangkok. You can take one of the many longtail boats and explore the surrounding canals and rivers. You can also find food stalls that have spread out from the riverbanks and stretched far into the surrounding streets all day long.

Ayutthaya (อยุธยา)—It is one of Thailand's historical and majestic highlights, and is only 86 km north of Bangkok. Ayutthaya became the second capital of Thailand, then known as the Kingdom of Ayutthaya. It is a truly impressive city with numerous magnificent temples and ruins concentrated in and around the city.

Kanchanaburi (กาญจนบุรี)—It has become a major tourist destination, with a focus on the outdoors due to its magnificent landscape and charming beauty. Only two hours from Bangkok, Kanchanaburi is accessible by road or rail, and is popular for fishing, rafting, canoeing, mountain biking, bird-watching, star-gazing, golfing, and elephant and jungle trekking.

Khao Yai National Park (อุทยานแห่งชาติเขาใหญ่)—It is a UNESCO World Heritage Site with the highest peak of 1,351 meters above sea level. Khao Yai is a year-round getaway destination just three hours' drive from Bangkok. It contains fertile forest, home and feeding ground for many kinds of animals. The park offers many trail options to choose from, 500 m up to 8 km long, all together over 50 km for hiking. There are also a number of waterfalls in the park, most of them easily accessible by vehicles and combined with a short walk.

Chiang Mai (เชียงใหม่) — It is a cultural and natural city in northern Thailand with ethnic diversity, a multitude of attractions and welcoming hospitality. Chiang Mai has over 300 Buddhist temples and hosts many Thai festivals, including Loy Krathong and Songkran. Chiang Mai is also blessed with pristine natural resources including mountains, waterfalls, and rivers. You can enjoy hill tribe trekking, river rafting, and elephant riding. Moreover, you can visit workshops where you can learn about the production of silk or silver, and purchase memorable, hand-crafted souvenirs. The Night Bazaar and Walking Street are also great places to buy your commonplace souvenirs at the absolute best prices.

Islands in Thailand

The islands off the coast of Thailand are famous throughout the world for their beautiful beaches and their gorgeous scenery. There are three main sets of islands in Thailand; those to the east of Bangkok are Koh Samet and Koh Chang; those in the southern Gulf of Thailand are Koh Samui, Koh Pha Ngan and Koh Tao; and those in the Andaman Sea are Koh Phi Phi, Koh Lanta, Koh Lipe, and Koh Tarutao. However, there are many more beautiful islands in Andaman Sea to choose from.

Hua-Hin and Cha-Am (หัวหิน-ชะอำ)—Hua-Hin is one of Thailand's premier beach resort towns on the Gulf of Thailand, is less than 200 km south of Bangkok, making it one of the most popular weekend getaway destinations for city residents. It features a beautiful, powdery sand beach, numerous seaside seafood restaurants, a lively night market, and numerous beach activities. Just down the coast at Takiab Bay you can take seaside horseback rides and visit a hilltop Buddhist temple with a spectacular view.

Cha-Am is located less than 200 km south of Bangkok and just 20 km north of Hua Hin. It is also a popular weekend destination for Bangkok residents who enjoy the sea, even if the sand is not as fine as at nearby Hua Hin. Cha-am also offers a number of beach activities, such as jet skiing and banana boat riding, and the seafood is as readily available and inexpensive as any beach town in Thailand.

Telling the time

Unfortunately, the common method of telling the time in Thai is rather complicated. The hours are as follows:

1 a.m. *dtii nèung* ตีหนึ่ง

2 a.m. *dtii sǒng* ตีสอง

3 a.m. *dtii sǎam* ตีสาม

4 a.m. *dtii sìi* ตีสี่

5 a.m. *dtii hâa* ตีห้า

6 a.m. *hòk mohng cháu* หกโมงเช้า

7 a.m. *jèt mohng cháu* เจ็ดโมงเช้า

8 a.m. *bpàet mohng cháu* แปดโมงเช้า

9 a.m. *gâu mohng cháu* เก้าโมงเช้า

10 a.m. *sìp mohng cháu* สิบโมงเช้า

11 a.m. *sìp-èt mohng cháu* สิบเอ็ดโมงเช้า

12 noon *thîang* เที่ยง

1 p.m. *bàai mohng* บ่ายโมง

2 p.m. *bàai sŏng mohng* บ่ายสองโมง

3 p.m. *bàai săam mohng* บ่ายสามโมง

4 p.m. *bàai sìi mohng* บ่ายสี่โมง or
sìi mohng yen สี่โมงเย็น

5 p.m. *hâa mohng* ห้าโมง or
hâa mohng yen ห้าโมงเย็น

6 p.m. *hòk mohng yen* หกโมงเย็น

7 p.m. *thûm* ทุ่ม or *nèung thûm* หนึ่งทุ่ม

8 p.m. *sŏng thûm* สองทุ่ม

9 p.m. *săam thûm* สามทุ่ม

10 p.m. *sìi thûm* สี่ทุ่ม

11 p.m. *hâa thûm* ห้าทุ่ม

12 midnight *thîang kheun* เที่ยงคืน

For the minutes after the hour, just add .... *naa-thii* นาที.

The 24-hour clock is also used for official purposes. In this system the number of hours is followed by *naa-li-gaa* นาฬิกา, and the minutes after the hour by *naa-thii* นาที (as above).

Days of the week

Monday *wan jan* วันจันทร์

Tuesday *wan angkhaan* วันอังคาร

Wednesday *wan phút* วันพุธ

Thursday *wan phareuhát* วันพฤหัส

Friday *wan sùk* วันศุกร์

Saturday *wan său* วันเสาร์

Sunday *wan aathít* วันอาทิตย์

Months of the year

January *mok-ga-raa-khom* มกราคม

February *gum-phaa-phan* กุมภาพันธ์

March *mii-naa-khom* มีนาคม

April *meh-săa-yon* เมษายน

May *phréut-saphaa-khom* พฤษภาคม

June *mí-thu-naa-yon* มิถุนายน

July *ga-rak-ga-daa-khom* กรกฎาคม

August *sĭng-hăa-khom* สิงหาคม

September *gan-yaa-yon* กันยายน

October *dtu-laa-khom* ตุลาคม

November *phréut-sa-ji-gaa-yon* พฤศจิกายน

December *than-waa-khom* ธันวาคม

Holidays

birthday *wan gèut* วันเกิด

a holiday *wan yùt* วันหยุด

"Father's Day," *Wan Phôr* วันพ่อ
that is, the King's birthday, 5 December

"Mother's Day," *Wan Mâe* วันแม่
the Queen's birthday, 12 August

Children's Day *Wan Dèk* วันเด็ก

Songkran Day *Wan Sŏngkhraan* วันสงกรานต์
(variable date, in April)

Thai kinship terms

Father *phôr* พ่อ

Mother *mâe* แม่

aunt (younger sister of mother) *náa* น้า

aunt (younger sister of father) *aa* อา

aunt (older sister of mother or father) *bpâa* ป้า

uncle (younger brother of mother) *náa* น้า

uncle (younger brother of father) *aa* อา

uncle (older brother of father or mother) *lung* ลุง

nephew *lăan-chaai* หลานชาย

niece *lăan săau* หลานสาว

grandmother (paternal) *yâa* ย่า

grandmother (maternal) *yaai* ยาย

grandfather (paternal) *bpùu* ปู่

grandfather (maternal) *dtaa* ตา

grandchild *lăan* หลาน

Some Thai proverbs

1. *Deun dtaam naai, măa mâi gàt.*
เดินตามผู้ใหญ่ หมาไม่กัด
"If you follow the master, dogs won't bite you."

In other words: If you do what you're told, you'll be okay. This alludes to the system of hierarchy in Thai society, and the demands for conformity to rules and regulations; the authorities will block you if you don't toe the line. If you have conflict you won't get anywhere. Underlings, no matter how well qualified, have to do what the bosses demand.

2. *Àap náam rórn maa gorn.* อาบน้ำร้อนมาก่อน
"To take a warm bath before you."

In other words: I was born before you, so I have more experience than you, and you had better take my word for it. Trust me! This is a bit like the English "I've had more hot dinners than you."

3. *Mái glâai fàng.* ไม้ใกล้ฝั่ง
"The log is near the bank."

In other words, my life is approaching its end (I have one foot in the grave), so you have to stand on your own feet, prepare yourself, set yourself up and get serious with your life. The image is of timber seasoning in a canal; if it is near the bank, it will soon be pulled out to be dried and milled.

4. **Măa gàt, yàa gàt dtòrp.** หมากัดอย่ากัดตอบ
   "When the dog bites, don't bite back."

In other words: don't lower yourself to fight with someone else, or don't stoop as low as your enemy. Don't bother to argue back. Note that the dog is an image of something low; the same applies to most animals, which are born in that state because of a lack of good deeds in former lives.

5. **Lûuk mái lòn mâi glai dtôn.** ลูกไม้หล่นไม่ไกลต้น
   "The fruit does not fall far from the tree."

English: Like father, like son.

6. **Duu cháang, hâi duu hăang; duu naang hâi duu mâe.**
   ดูช้างให้ดูหาง ดูนางให้ดูแม่
   "Looking at an elephant, you should check its tail, and when looking at a girl, you should check her mother."

In other words, "like mother, like daughter."

7. **Jàp bplaa sŏng meu.** จับปลาสองมือ
   "Catching fish with two hands."

This means catching one fish in each hand, and losing both. In other words, it is better to focus on what you are doing, and do it well.

Emergency expressions

Sorry! (also: **excuse me, pardon?**) *Khŏr thôht* ขอโทษ

Help! *Chûai dûai!* ช่วยด้วย

Fire! *Fai mâi!* ไฟไหม้

Police! *Dtamrùat! Dtamrùat!* ตำรวจ

Thief! *Khamoi!* ขโมย

Look out! (beware): *Rawang!* ระวัง

Don't (do that): *Yàa!* อย่า

Just a moment! *Dĭau gòrn.* เดี๋ยวก่อน

No! (that's not right): *Mâi châi!* ไม่ใช่

Stop! *Yùt!* หยุด

That's enough! *Pho láeu.* พอแล้ว

What a pity! *Sĭa dai.* เสียดาย

It's okay (I don't mind): *Mâi bpen rai.* ไม่เป็นไร

Thanks a lot! *Khop khun mâak!* ขอบคุณมาก

Right! (correct) *Châi!* ใช่

That's great! *Dii mâak!* ดีมาก

What fun! *Sanùk!* สนุก

That's odd! *Bplàek!* แปลก

What does... mean? .... *Bplae wâa à-rai?* แปลว่าอะไร

See you again! *Phóp gan mài.* พบกันใหม่

English-Thai Wordlist

about, concerning, relating to
   rêuang เรื่อง
about, approximately (informal)
   rau-rau ราว ราว, (formal)
   bpra-maan ประมาณ
above **nĕua** เหนือ
across **trong-khâam** ตรงข้าม
accident **ù-bàt-tì-hèt** อุบัติเหตุ
accommodation **thîi-phák** ที่พัก
ache, to **bpùat** ปวด
add **sài, phôem** ใส่, เพิ่ม
addicted **dtìt** ติด
address **thîi-yòu** ที่อยู่
adorable **nâa-rák** น่ารัก
advise **náe-nam** แนะนำ
afraid/scared **glua** กลัว
afternoon, in the **dtorn bàai**
   ตอนบ่าย
again, anew **mài** ใหม่, (another
   time) **ìik khráng** อีกครั้ง
age; to be aged… **aayú'** อายุ
ago **thîi-láew** ที่แล้ว
agree (with someone) **hĕn-dûay**
   เห็นด้วย
AIDS **rôhk AIDS** โรคเอดส์ (pron.
   ehd เอด)
air **aa-kàat** อากาศ
airplane **khrûeang-bin** เครื่องบิน

airport **sanăam-bin** สนามบิน
alcohol, liquor **lâo** เหล้า
all, at all **leui** เลย
allergic/allergy **pháe** แพ้
almost **kùeap** เกือบ
alone (be by oneself) **khon-diaw**
   คนเดียว
already **láew** แล้ว
also, as well, too **dûay** ด้วย
ambulance **rót-phá-yaa-baan**
   รถพยาบาล
American **amerigan** อเมริกัน
amphetamines **yaa bâa** ยาบ้า
amulet **phrá' khrêuang** พระเครื่อง
amusing/funny **tà-lòk** ตลก
and **láe'** และ
angry **kròt** โกรธ
animal **sàt** สัตว์
annoy **ram-khaan** รำคาญ
another, more **ìik** อีก
anthem, national **phlehng châat**
   เพลงชาติ
any-, anything **à-rai gôr dâi** อะไร
   ก็ได้; anyone **khrai gôr dâi** ใคร
   ก็ได้; any time **meua-rài gôr dâi**
   เมื่อไหร่ก็ได้; any kind **thúk**
   yàang ทุกอย่าง
apartment **apaatmen** อพาร์ตเม็น

apologize, to **khŏr thôht** ขอโทษ;
  apology **kham khŏr thôht**
  คำขอโทษ

appearance **nâa-taa** หน้าตา

apple **aepen** แอปเปิล

apply (for a job) **sà-màk** สมัคร

appointment **nát-măay** นัดหมาย

appreciate/thanks **khàwp-khun**
  ขอบคุณ

appropriate/suitable **màw-sŏm**
  เหมาะสม

arm **khăen** แขน

arrange **jàt-kaan** จัดการ

arrive, to **thĕung** ถึง

article, thing, goods **khŏrng** ของ

ask, to (a question) **thăam (wâa)**
  ถามว่า

assist **châuy** ช่วย

asthma **aesmâa** หอบหืด

at **thîi** ที่

Australia **áwt-sà-tre-lia** ออสเตรเลีย

available, free (not busy) **wâang** ว่าง

back (side) **khâng lăng** ข้างหลัง;
  to go back, return **glàp** กลับ;
  to go back on one's word **glàp
  kham** กลับคำ

backache **bpùat lăng** ปวดหลัง

bad **leho** เลว

bag (handbag, suitcase) **gra-bpău**
  กระเป๋า

banana **glûay** กล้วย

bank (of river) **fàng (náam)** ฝั่ง(น้ำ)

bank (for money) **thana-khaan**
  ธนาคาร

banknote **bank** แบงค์/**thana-bat**
  ธนบัตร (counting word: **bai** ใบ)

barber **châang-tàt-phŏm** ช่างตัดผม

bath, to take a bath **àap náam**
  อาบน้ำ

bathroom **hông-náam** ห้องน้ำ

bathtub **àang-àap-náam**
  อ่างอาบน้ำ

be, to (not translated in many cases);
  to be there, present **yùu** อยู่

beach **chaai-hàat** ชายหาด

beat (to strike) **tii** ตี

beautiful **sŭai** สวย

because **phró'-wâa** เพราะว่า

bed **dtiang** เตียง

bedroom **hâwng-nawn** ห้องนอน

bed sheet **phâa-pou-thîi-nawn** ผ้า
  ปูที่นอน

beef **néua** เนื้อ

beer **bia** เบียร์

before **kàwn** ก่อน

begin **rôem** เริ่ม

behind **khâang-lăng** ข้างหลัง

believe, to **chêua** เชื่อ; believable
  nâa-chêua น่าเชื่อ

beside **khâng** ข้าง

best **dii-thîi-sùt** ดีที่สุด

better **dii-kwàa** ดีกว่า

between **rá-wàang** ระหว่าง

140

bicycle *jàk-krà-yaan* จักรยาน

big *yài* ใหญ่

bird *nók* นก

birthday *wan gèut* วันเกิด

bit, a *nít nòi* นิดหน่อย

black *sǐi dam* สีดำ

blanket *phâa-hòm* ผ้าห่ม

blood *lûeat* เลือด

blouse *sêua phûu yǐng* เสื้อสีดำ

blue (dark) *sǐi-náam-ngoen* สีน้ำเงิน

blue (light) *sǐi-fáa* สีฟ้า

boat *reua* เรือ

body *râang-kaay, tua* ร่างกาย, ตัว

boil *tôm* ต้ม

book *nǎngsěu* หนังสือ

book, to *jorng* จอง

boring *nâa-bèua* น่าเบื่อ

born, to be *gèut* เกิด

borrow *yuem* ยืม

boss, head *hǔa nâa* หัวหน้า

bottle *khwàt* ขวด

bowl *chaam* ชาม

boxing *muay* มวย;
   boxer *nák-muay* นักมวย

boyfriend *faen* แฟน

breakfast *ahǎan cháau* อาหารเช้า

bride *jâo-sǎaw* เจ้าสาว

bridegroom *jâo-bàaw* เจ้าบ่าว

bridge *sà-phaan* สะพาน

bring up/raise (children) *líang* เลี้ยง

British *anggrìt* อังกฤษ

brother (older) *phîi* พี่; (younger) *nóng* น้อง

brothers and sisters (siblings) *phîi-nóng* พี่น้อง

brother-in-law (older) *phîi khěui* พี่เขย; (younger) *nóng khěui* น้องเขย

brown *sǐi-náam-taan* สีน้ำตาล

brush, to (hair) *wǐi* หวี

Buddha image *phrá' phúttharûup* พระพุทธรูป

building (structure) *tùek* ตึก

burn *phǎo* เผา

bus *rót bas, rót meh* รถบัส, รถเมล์

bus station *sathaanii rót bas* สถานีรถบัส

business *thú-rá'* ธุระ

but *tàe* แต่

butter *noei* เนย

buy, to *séu* ซื้อ

by (means of) *doi* โดย

cabinet *tôu* ตู้

calculate, to *khít* คิด

calculator *khrûeang-khít-lêk* เครื่องคิดเลข

call, to; to be called *rîak (wâa)* เรียกว่า (*see also* telephone)

calm, cool-headed *jai-yen* ใจเย็น

can, able to *dâi* ได้

Canada *khae-naa-daa* แคนาดา

cancel *yók-lôek* ยกเลิก

cancer *má-reng* มะเร็ง

candle *thian* เทียน

car *rót, rót yon* รถ, รถยนต์

careful *rá-wang* ระวัง

carry (in the hands) *hîw, thěu* หิ้ว, ถือ

cash *ngeun sòt* เงินสด

cat *maeo* แมว

catch, to (a disease) *dtìt rôhk* ติดโรค

cattle *wua* วัว

celebrate, to *chàlǎwng* ฉลอง

cell phone *mue-thǔe* มือถือ

ceremony, festival, celebration *ngaan* งาน

chair *kôa-îi* เก้าอี้

change (small money) *ngeun thorn* เงินทอน

charter, to *mǎu* เหมา

chat, to *khui* คุย

cheap *thùuk* ถูก

cheap, easy to get (woman) *jai-ngâai* ใจง่าย

check (bank document) *chék* เช็ค

chicken *gài* ไก่

child (young person) *dèk* เด็ก; (someone's offspring) *lûuk* ลูก

chili *phrík* พริก

Chinese *jiin* จีน

chopstick(s) *dtagìap* ตะเกียบ

cigarette *bù-rìi* บุหรี่

city, large town *mueang* เมือง

class *rian* เรียน

clean (adjective) *sà-àat* สะอาด

clean, to (teeth) *bpraeng fan* แปรงฟัน

clever *chà-làat* ฉลาด

climate *aagàat* อากาศ

clinic *kliinik* คลีนิค

close *glâi* ใกล้

cloth *phâa* ผ้า

clothes *phâa* ผ้า

cloud *mêhk* เมฆ

coconut *má-práow* มะพร้าว

coconut milk *krà-thí* กะทิ

coffee *gaafae* กาแฟ

cold *nǎau* หนาว

cold, to have a cold *bpen wàt* เป็นหวัด

color *sǐi* สี

comb *wǐi* หวี

come, to *maa* มา

comfortable *sabai* สบาย

comic book *nǎngsěu khaa-thuun* หนังสือการ์ตูน

company *baw-rí-sàt* บริษัท

compete, to *khàeng* แข่ง

complain, to *bòn* บ่น; complaint *kham-bòn* คำบ่น

completely *khròp* ครบ, *tháng-mòt* ทั้งหมด

compose, to (write, a song) *dtàeng*

phlehng แต่งเพลง; composer, songwriter *nák dtàeng phlehng* นักแต่งเพลง

computer *cawm-phíew-tôe* คอมพิวเตอร์

condominium *kondoh* คนโด; *hông-chút* ห้องชุด

confident *mân-jai* มั่นใจ

confused *ngong* งง

connect *tàw* ต่อ

consideration (for others) *greng-jai* เกรงใจ

consult, to (doctor, dentist) *hǎa* หา

control (something) *khûap-khum* ควบคุม

convenient *sà-dùak* สะดวก

cook, to (prepare food) *tham ahǎan* ทำอาหาร

cool *yen* เย็น

corn *khâo-phôt* ข้าวโพด

corner *mum* มุม

correct, right *thùuk* ถูก

cost (price) *raa-khaa* ราคา

cotton cloth *phâa fâai* ผ้าฝ้าย

cough, to *ai* ไอ

country *prà-thêt* ประเทศ

court (of law) *sǎan* ศาล

cow *wua* วัว

crab *pou* ปู

crash *chon* ชน

crazy, mad *bâa* บ้า

create/build, to *sâang* สร้าง

credit card *bàt kredít* บัตรเครดิต

cross (angry) *gròht* โกรธ; *mohǒ* โมโห

cross, to (street) *khâam* ข้าม

cry, to (weep) *rórng hâi* ร้องไห้

cry, to cry out *rórng* ร้อง

cup *thûai* ถ้วย

curry *gaeng* แกง

cushion (pillow) *mǎwn* หมอน

cut *tàt* ตัด

cut (injure) *phlǎe* แผล

cute *nâa-rák* น่ารัก

dance, to *dtênram* เต้น; dancer *nák dtênram* นักเต้น; classical Thai dance *ram Thai* รำไทย; folk dance (in circles) *ram wong* รำวง

danger/dangerous *an-tà-raay* อันตราย

dark (of color) *khêm* เข้ม

dark (night) *mûet* มืด

dark (complexion) *khlám* คล้ำ

daughter *lûuk sǎau* ลูกสาว

day *wan* วัน

dead *taay* ตาย

debt *nîi* หนี้

deceased (to pass away) *sǐa chiiwít* เสียชีวิต

decorate, to *dtàeng* แต่ง

deep *lúek* ลึก

delay *cháa* ช้า

delete *lóp* ลบ

delicious *à-ròi* อร่อย

deliver *sòng* ส่ง

dentist (formal) *than-tà-phâet* ทันตแพทย์; (common) *măw-fan* หมอฟัน

depart *àwk-jàak* ออกจาก

department, section *phanàek* แผนก

department store *hâang* ห้าง

desk *tóe* โต๊ะ

dessert *khà-nŏm* ขนม

dessert, sweet *khăwng-wăan* ของหวาน

diarrhea *thórng deun/rûang* ท้องเดิน/ท้องร่วง

die, to *dtai* ตาย

difficult *yâak* อยาก

dinner *ahăan yen* อาหารเย็น

dirty *sòk-gà-bpròk* สกปรก

disappear, to *hăai* หาย

disco *disko* ดีสโก

discount *lót* ลด

disease *rôhk* โรค

dish, plate *jaan* จาน

disheartened, to lose heart *jai-sĭa* ใจเสีย

dislike *mâi-châwp* ไม่ชอบ

district *ampheu (amphur)* อำเภอ

dive *dam-náam* ดำน้ำ

divorce, to; to be divorced *yàa* หย่า

dizzy *wian-hŭa* เวียนหัว

do *tham* ทำ

doctor *mŏr* หมอ

don't! *yàa* อย่า

dog *măa* หมา

door *prà-tou* ประตู

double room *hông khûu* ห้องคู่; double bed *dtiang khûu* เตียงคู่

down *long* ลง

downstairs *khâng lâng* ข้างล่าง

draw (a picture), to *wâat* วาด

dream *făn* ฝัน

dress, to get dressed *dtàeng-dtua* แต่งตัว

drink, to *dèum* ดื่ม; *gin* (informal) กิน

drive *khàp* ขับ

drug *yaa* ยา

drugged, doped *mau yaa* เมายา

drunk *mau* เมา; *mau-lâu* เมาเหล้า

dry *hâeng* แห้ง

duck *pèt* เป็ด

durian *thurian* ทุเรียน

each other *gan* กัน

earache *bpùat hŭa* ปวดหัว

ears *hŭu* หู

easy *ngâai* ง่าย

eat, to *gin* กิน

edge (of river) *rim* ริม

egg *khài* ไข่

elbow *khâw-sàwk* ข้อศอก

electric, electricity *fai-fáa* ไฟฟ้า

elephant *cháang* ช้าง

embassy *sathǎan thûut* สถานทูต

emergency *chùk-chǒen* ฉุกเฉิน

empty *wàang* ว่าง

end (ending) *jòp* จบ

engaged (to be married) *mân* หมั้น

English (language) *phaasǎa anggrìt* ภาษาอังกฤษ

enjoy, to (oneself) *sànùk* สนุก

enough, sufficient *phaw* พอ

enter, to *khâo* เข้า

entrance *thaang-khâo* ทางเข้า

envelope *sawng* ซอง

equal *thâo* เท่า

errand *thù-rá* ธุระ

ethics, moral code *sǐinlatham* ศีลธรรม

evening *dtawn-yen* ตอนเย็น

ever *khoei* เคย

every *thúk* ทุก

everyday *thúk-wan* ทุกวัน

everyone *thúk-khon* ทุกคน

everything *thúk yàang* ทุกอย่าง

exchange, to (money) *lâek* แลก

excited *jai-dtên* ใจเต้น; *dtèun-dtên* ตื่นเต้น

excuse me *khǒr thôht* ขอโทษ

exercise, to *àwk-kam-lang kaay* ออกกำลังกาย

exit *thaang òrk* ทางออก

expensive *phaeng* แพง

experience *prà-sòp-kaan* ประสบการณ์

express, urgent *dùan* ด่วน

extra *phí-sèt* พิเศษ

extremely *thîi-sùt* ที่สุด

eye *dtaa* ตา

face *nǎa* หน้า

faint, to; to feel faint *bpen lom* เป็นลม

fall, to *dtòk* ตก

family *khrâwp-khrua* ครอบครัว

fan *phát-lom* พัดลม

fancy *rǔu* หรู

far *glai* ไกล

fare, rate, tariff *khâa* ค่า

farmer *chaaw-naa* ชาวนา

fast *reo* เร็ว

fat *ûan* อ้วน

father *phôr* พ่อ

father-in-law *phôr dtaa* พ่อตา (wife's father); *phôr phǔa* พ่อผัว (husband's father)

fear *glua* กลัว

fee *khâa* ค่า

feel *róu-sùek* รู้สึก

female *yǐng* หญิง

fever, to have a fever *bpen-khâi* เป็นไข้

field, lawn *sà-nǎam* สนาม

field, paddy *naa* นา

fight *sôu* สู้

finger *níw* นิ้ว

finished (done) *sèt* เสร็จ; (used up) *mòt* หมด

fish *bplaa* ปลา

five *hâa* ห้า

flashlight, torch *fai-chăay* ไฟฉาย

flesh, meat *núea* เนื้อ

flight (an airline) *thîaw-bin* เที่ยวบิน

flirt *jùip* จีบ

float *loy* ลอย

flood *nám-thûam* น้ำท่วม

floor (level) *chán* ชั้น

flour *pâeng* แป้ง

flower *dàwk-mái* ดอกไม้

flu *khâi wàt* ไข้หวัด

follow, to *dtaam* ตาม

fond of, attracted to *dùit jai* ติดใจ

food *ahăan* อาหาร; Thai food *ahăan Thai* อาหารไทย

foot *tháo* เท้า

football (soccer) *fútbon* ฟุตบอล

forbid, to; forbidden *hâam* ห้าม

foreigner (Westerner) *faràng* ฝรั่ง

forget, to *leum* ลืม

fortune-teller *mŏr duu* หมอดู

four *sìi* สี่

French *faràngsèt* ฝรั่งเศส

fried rice *khâau phàt* ข้าวผัด

friend *phêuan* เพื่อน; to be friends *bpen phêuan gan* เป็นเพื่อนกัน

from *jàak* จาก

front *khâng nâa* ข้างหน้า

fruit (in general) *phŏnlamái* ผลไม้

fry *thâwt* ทอด

full, to have eaten enough *ìm* อิ่ม

fun, amusement, a good time *sanùk* สนุก

funny, comical *dtalòk* ตลก

funeral *ngaan sòp* งานศพ

future *à-naa-khót* อนาคต

garage (for parking) *rong-rót* โรงรถ

garbage/rubbish/trash *khà-yà* ขยะ

garden, yard *sŭan* สวน

garlic *krà-thiam* กระเทียม

gas, gasoline, petrol *nám-man* น้ำมัน

gas station *pám-nám-man* ปั๊มน้ำมัน

generous *jai-dee* ใจดี

German *yeraman* เยอรมัน

get (receive) *dâi* ได้

get up *tùen-nawn* ตื่นนอน

get well *hăay* หาย

ghost *phĭi* ผี

gift/present *khăwng-khwăn* ของขวัญ

ginger *khĭng* ขิง

girl (child) *dèk-phôu-yĭng* เด็กผู้หญิง

girlfriend *faen* แฟน

give, to *hâi* ให้

glass *gâeu* แก้ว

glasses *wâen-dtaa* แว่นตา

go, to *bpai* ไป; to go up *khêun* ขึ้น; to go down *long* ลง

good *dii* ดี; goodness *khwaam dii* ความดี

goodbye *laa-gòr* ลาก่อน; *báai-baai* บ๊ายบาย; *(sa)wàtdii* สวัสดี

green *sĭi khĭau* สีเขียว

grape *à-ngùn* องุ่น

grass *yâa* หญ้า

grateful *khàwp-khun* ขอบคุณ

gray, grey *sĭi-thao* สีเทา

grill *yàang* ย่าง

group *klùm* กลุ่ม

guava *fà-ràng* ฝรั่ง

guest (visitor) *khàek* แขก

guitar *gii-dtâa* กีตาร์

hair *phŏm* ผม

half *khrêung* ครึ่ง

hand *meu* มือ

handsome *lòr* หล่อ

happy *dii jai* ดีใจ; *mii khaam-sùk* มีความสุข

hard (heavy, work) *nàk* หนัก; (difficult) *yâak* ยาก

hat, cap *mùak* หมวก

hate *klìat* เกลียด

have, to *mii* มี

he *khău* เขา

head *hŭa* หัว

headache *bpùat hŭa* ปวดหัว

heal *rák-sǎa* รักษา

health, in good health *sabai dii* สบายดี

hear *dâi-yin* ได้ยิน

heart (anatomical) *hŭa-jai* หัวใจ

hello *(sa)wàtdii* สวัสดี

here *thîi nîi* ที่นี่

high *sŭung* สูง

him *khăo* เขา

his *khăwng-khăo* ของเขา

hit *tii* ตี

holiday, trip *thîau* เที่ยว; (day with no work) *wan yùt* วันหยุด

holy, sacred *sàksìt* ศักดิ์สิทธิ์

home *bâan* บ้าน; at home *thîi bâan* ที่บ้าน; to go home *glàp bâan* กลับบ้าน

homework *kaan-bâan* การบ้าน

honey *náam-phûeng* น้ำผึ้ง

hope *wăng* หวัง

horrible (frightening) *nâa-klua* น่ากลัว

hospital *rohng phayabaan* โรงพยาบาล

hot (temperature) *rórn* ร้อน

hotel *rongraem* โรงแรม

hour *chûa-mong* ชั่วโมง

house *bâan* บ้าน

how? (informal) *yang-ngai* ยังไง,
    (formal) *yàang-rai* อย่างไร

how many? *gìi* กี่

huge *yài* ใหญ่

humid *chúen* ชื้น

humorous, funny *tà-lòk* ตลก

hundred *róoi* ร้อย

hurt, to (sore) *jèp* เจ็บ

hurt (injured), sore *jèp* เจ็บ

hurt, offended *jèp-jai* เจ็บใจ

husband (informal) *phŭa* ผัว;
    (formal) *sǎamii* สามี

I (man speaking) *phŏm* ผม;
    (woman speaking, informal)
    chǎn ฉัน, (woman speaking,
    formal) *dichǎn* ดิฉัน

ice *nám-khǎeng* น้ำแข็ง

if *thâa* ถ้า

ill/sick *mâi-sà-baay* ไม่สบาย

image *rôup-phâap* รูปภาพ

immediately *than-thii* ทันที

impatient *jai-ráwn* ใจร้อน

important *sǎm-khan* สำคัญ

in, inside *nai* ใน

in front *khâang-nâa* ข้างหน้า

in order to *phûea* เพื่อ

incense stick *thôup* ธูป

inconvenient *mâi-sà-dùak*
    ไม่สะดวก

incorrect, wrong *phìt* ผิด

infected *dtìt chéua* ติดเชื้อ

inform *jâeng* แจ้ง

information, data *khâw-moun*
    ข้อมูล

inject, to *chìit* ฉีด

injured *bàat-jèp* บาดเจ็บ

insects *má-laeng* แมลง

inside *khâang-nai* ข้างใน

installments, in *phòn sòng* ผ่อนส่ง

interested, absorbed (in) *sǒn-jai*
    สนใจ

interesting *nâa-sǒnjai* น่าสนใจ

internet *in-toe-nèt* อินเตอร์เน็ต

interpret/translate *plae* แปล

interpreter *lâam* ล่าม

intersection *sìi-yâek* สี่แยก

interview *sǎm-phâat* สัมภาษณ์

introduce *náe-nam* แนะนำ

invite, to *cheun* เชิญ

is *pen, yòu* เป็น, อยู่

island *kàw* เกาะ

it (a specific thing) *man* มัน
    (otherwise not translated)

Italy *ì-taa-lǐi* อิตาลี

itchy *khan* คัน

item *khôr* ข้อ

jail *khúk* คุก

jam *yaem* แยม

Japanese *yîi-bpùn* ญี่ปุ่น

jar (a large water jar) *òng* โอ่ง

joke, to *phûut lên* พูดเล่น

journalist *nák-khàaw* นักข่าว

juice *nám-phǒn-lá-mái* น้ำผลไม้

jump *krà-dòt* กระโดด

jungle *pàa* ป่า

just now *phôeng* เพิ่ง

kale *khá-náa* คะน้า

keep *kèp* เก็บ

kettle *kaa-nám* กาน้ำ

key (for a room) *kun-jae* กุญแจ

kick *tè* เตะ

kid (child) *dèk* เด็ก

kidney *tai* ไต

kill, to *khâa* ฆ่า

kilo *gi-loh* กิโล

kilometer *gi-loh* กิโล, *gi-lohmét* กิโลเมตร

kind, sort, variety *yàang* อย่าง

kind(hearted) *jai dii* ดีใจ

kindly, please *garunaa* กรุณา

king *phrá' jâau yùu hǔa* พระเจ้าอยู่หัว, ในหลวง

kiss, to *jòup* จูบ

kitchen *khrua* ครัว

knee *khào* เข่า

knife *mîit* มีด

know, to (informal) *rúu* รู้; (formal) *sâap* ทราบ

know, to (be acquainted) *rúujàk* รู้จัก

knowledge *khwaam rúu* ความรู้

lamp *khom* โคมไฟ

land, property *thîi-din* ที่ดิน

lane *soi* ซอย

language *phaasǎa* ภาษา

large, big *yâi* ใหญ่

last (week etc.) *thîi láeu* ที่แล้ว

late (behind time) *cháa* ช้า

late (in the morning) *sǎi* สาย

late at night *dtorn dtèuk* ตอนดึก

laugh *hǔa-ráw* หัวเราะ

laundry *sák-phâa* ซักผ้า

lawyer *thá-naay-khwaam* ทนายความ

laxative *yaa thàai* ยาถ่าย

leak *rûa* รั่ว

learn, study *rian* เรียน

leather *nǎng* หนัง

leave, to (go out) *òrk* ออก (from: *jàak* จาก)

left (hand) *sáai* ซ้าย

leg *khǎa* ขา

lemongrass *tà-khrái* ตะไคร้

lend *hâi-yuem* ให้ยืม

let's go! *bpai!* ไป; *bpai-gan-theu* ไปกันเถอะ

letter *jòtmǎai* จดหมาย

level (floor) *chán* ชั้น

lie down, to *norn* นอน

life *chii-wít* ชีวิต

lift (elevator) *líp* ลิบ

light (of color) *àwn* อ่อน

light (bright) *sà-wàang* สว่าง

light (lamp) *fai* ไฟ

like, similar *měuan* เหมือน

like, to; have a liking for *chôrp* ชอบ

like that, in that way *yàang nán* อย่างนั้น; like this *yàang nǔ* อย่างนี้

listen, to (to) *fang* ฟัง

little, small *lék* เล็ก

little, a little *nòi* หน่อย

live, to; to be at a location, dwell *yùu* อยู่

long (time) *naan* นาน

look, to look after, care for *duu lae* ดูแล; to look for *hǎa* หา

lose, be defeated *phâe* แพ้

lost *hǎay* หาย

lot, a lot of (informal) *yéuk* เยอะ; (formal) *mâak* มาก

loud *dang* ดัง

love *rák* รัก

lovely, cute, attractive *nâa-rák* น่ารัก

luck, good *chohk dii* โชคดี

luggage/bag/suitcase *krà-pǎo* กระเป๋า

lunch *ahǎan thîang* อาหารเที่ยง

lyrics (words of song) *néua phlehng* เนื้อเพลง

make, to *tham* ทำ

make-up, to put on make-up *dtàeng nâa* แต่งหน้า

male *chaai* ชาย

man/men *phôu-chaay* ผู้ชาย

manager *phôu-jàt-kaan* ผู้จัดการ

mango *ma-mûang* มะม่วง

mangosteen *mang-khút* มังคุด

manners (etiquette/behavior) *maa-rá-yâat* มารยาท

many, several, various *lǎai* หลาย

map *phǎen-thîi* แผนที่

market *dta-làat* ตลาด

marry, to; to be married *dtàeng-ngaan* (to: *gàp*) แต่งงานกับ

massage *nûat* นวด

may I have… *khǒr* ขอ

mean, to mean *bplae (wâa)* แปลว่า

mean, selfish *jai-dam* ใจดำ

measure *wát* วัด

meat/flesh *núea* เนื้อ

medicine *yaa* ยา

medium (not too much) *bpaan-glaang* ปานกลาง

meet, to meet *phóp* พบ

meeting, conference *bpra-chum* ประชุม

melody, tune *thamnorng phlehng* ทำนองเพลง

menu *menu* เมนู

merit (religious) *bun* บุญ

middle, center *glaang* กลาง

migraine *maigren* ไมเกรน

milk *nom* นม

million *láan* ล้าน

mince (meat/pork) *sàp* สับ

mind *jai* ใจ

mine (female) *khǎwng-chǎn* ของฉัน; (male) *khǎwng-phǒm* ของผม

ministry (government ministry) *krà-suang* กระทรวง

minute *naathii* นาที

miss, to (think of) *khít thěung* คิดถึง

miss (title) *naang sǎau* นางสาว

mist, fog *mǎwk* หมอก

mix/blend, to *phà-sǒm* ผสม

mobile phone *mue-thǔe* มือถือ

moment, auspicious *rêuk* ฤกษ์

money *ngeun* เงิน

monk *phrá'* พระ

month *deuan* เดือน

morning *dtorn cháau* ตอนเช้า

most, the (-est) *thîi sùt* ที่สุด

mother *mâe* แม่

mother-in-law (wife's mother) *mâe yaai* แม่ยาย; (husband's mother) *mâe phǔa* แม่ผัว, *mâe sǎamii* แม่สามี

motorcycle *motersai* มอเตอร์ไซ จักรยานยนต์

mountain *phu-khǎu* ภูเขา

movie, film *nǎng* หนัง; movie theater *rohng nǎng* โรงหนัง

much, a lot, very *mâak* มาก

museum *phi-phít-ta-phan* พิพิธภัณฑ์

music *don-dtrii* ดนตรี

nail (finger, toe) *lép* เล็บ

name *chêu* ชื่อ; family name *naam sagun* นามสกุล; first name *chêu jing* ชื่อจริง; nickname *chêu lên* ชื่อเล่น

nation, nationality; national *châat* ชาติ

naughty *son* ซน

near *klâi* ใกล้

necessary *jam-bpen* จำเป็น

neck *khǎw* คอ

need, to *dtông* ต้อง; no need *mâi dtông* ไม่ต้อง

neighbor *phêuan bâan* เพื่อนบ้าน

new *mài* ใหม่

newspaper *nǎngsěu phim* หนังสือพิมพ์

New Zealand *niw-sii-laen* นิวซีแลนด์

nice/good *dii* ดี

nickname *chêu-lên* ชื่อเล่น

night, at night *glaang kheun* กลางคืน

no (I don't agree) *mâi châi* ไม่ใช่; (I don't want it) *mâi au* ไม่เอา

noise/a sound *sǐang* เสียง

noisy/loud noise *sǐang-dang* เสียงดัง

noodles **kŭay-tîaw** ก๋วยเตี๋ยว

noon, at noon **dtorn thîang**
ตอนเที่ยง

north-east **isăan** อิสาน

nose **jà-mòuk** จมูก

not **mâi** ไม่

not very **mâi khôi** ไม่ค่อย

novice (Buddhist) **nehn** เณร

now **tawn-nîi** ตอนนี้

number (in street; telephone) **ber**
เบอร์; (figure) **lêhk** เลข

nun **mâe chii** แม่ชี

nurse **phá-yaa-baan** พยาบาล

object, thing **sìng** สิ่ง

of, belong to **khăwng** ของ

often **bòi** บ่อย

office **óp-fít** ออฟฟิต

oil **nám-man** น้ำมัน

old-fashioned, traditional **bo-raan**
โบราณ

on (on top of) **bon** บน

one **nèung** หนึ่ง

one way **thîaw-diaw** เที่ยวเดียว

onion **hŭa-hăwm** หัวหอม

open, turn on **pòet** เปิด

opposite **trong-khâam** ตรงข้าม

or **rĕu** หรือ; or not **rĕu bplàu**
หรือเปล่า

orange **sôm** ส้ม

order **sang** สั่ง

other **ùen** อื่น

our **khăwng-rao** ของเรา

outside **khâang-nâwk** ข้างนอก

oven **tao-òp** เตาอบ

overseas **tàang-prà-thêt**
ต่างประเทศ

ox **wua** วัว

page (in a book) **nâa** หน้า

pain/painful **jèp** เจ็บ

pair **kôu** คู่

pajamas/pyjamas **chút-nawn**
ชุดนอน

palace, royal **phrá'-raat-cha-wang**
พระราชวัง

pants, trousers **gang-gehng**
กางเกง

paper **gra-dàat** กระดาษ

parents **phôr-mâe** พ่อแม่

passport **năngsĕu deun thaang**
หนังสือเดินทาง

pay, to **jàai** จ่าย

peanut **thùa** ถั่ว

pen **pàak-kaa** ปากกา

pencil **din-săw** ดินสอ

people **khon** คน

pepper (chili pepper) **phrík** พริก

per, by the... **lá'** ละ

perform, to; to show, display
sa-daeng แสดง

performance, exhibition **gaan**
sa-daeng การแสดง

performer **phûu sa-daeng** ผู้แสดง

perfume *nám-hǎwm* น้ำหอม

person *khon* คน

personal *sǔan dtua* ส่วนตัว

pet (animal) *sàt-líang* สัตว์เลี้ยง

petrol/gasoline *nám-man* น้ำมัน

pick up, to (take) *gèp* เก็บ; (go and meet) *ráp* รับ

pig *mǔu* หมู

pill(s) *yaa* ยา

pillow/cushion *mǎwn* หมอน

pineapple *sàp-pà-rót* สับปะรด

pink *sǔu-chom-phou* สีชมพู

place *thîi* ที่; place to sit *thîi nâng* ที่นั่ง

plane *khrêuang bin* เครื่องบิน

plate *jaan* จาน

play, drama *la-khorn* ละคร

play, to *lên* เล่น

pleased, glad *yin dii* ยินดี

pleased, delighted *cheun-jai* ชื่นใจ

poet *ga-wii* กวี

police station *sa-thǎa-nii dtam rùat* สถานีตำรวจ

pork *mǔu* หมู

port, harbor *thâa-ruea* ท่าเรือ

post office *prai-sà-nii* ไปรษณีย์

post, mail *jòt-mǎay* จดหมาย

pot (for rice) *môr* หม้อ

powder (talcum) *bpaeng* แป้ง

precept, moral *sǐin* ศีล

pregnant *mii thórng* มีท้อง

prepare, make ready *triam* เตรียม

prescription (for medicine) *bai sàng yaa* ใบสั่งยา

present (gift) *khǎwng-khwǎn* ของขวัญ

pretty *sǔay* สวย

price *raa-khaa* ราคา

primary (school) *bpra-thǒm* ประถม

prize/reward *raang-wan* รางวัล

problem *pan-hǎa* ปัญหา

professor *aa-jaan* อาจารย์

promise *sǎn-yaa* สัญญา

proud, to be *phoum-jai* ภูมิใจ

province *jangwàt (changwat)* จังหวัด

pull, to *dueng* ดึง

punctual, on time *trong-we-laa* ตรงเวลา

purple *sǐi-mûang* สีม่วง

purse *krá-pǎo* กระเป๋า

put, to put in, add *sài* ใส่

pyjamas *chút norn* ชุดนอน

quarrel, to *thaló' gan* ทะเลาะกัน

queen *phrá' raa-chi-nii* พระราชินี

question *kham-thǎam* คำถาม

quickly *reo* เร็ว

quiet *ngîap* เงียบ

quit/give up *lôek* เลิก

quit/resign *laa-àwk* ลาออก

rabbit *krà-tàay* กระต่าย

radio **wít-thá-yú** วิทยุ

rain **fǒn** ฝน

raise, breed **líang** เลี้ยง

rash **phùen** ผื่น

rat/mouse **nǒu** หนู

reach, to **thěung** ถึง

really (believe me!) **jing-jing!** จริง จริง

reasonable **mó'sǒm** เหมาะสม

recover, to (from illness) **hǎai** หาย

red **sǐi daeng** สีแดง

reduce, to (lower) **lót** ลด

refrigerator **tôu-yen** ตู้เย็น

region (of Thailand) **phâak** ภาค

regret (to feel sorry) **sǐa-jai** เสียใจ

relatives (family) **yâat** ญาติ

religious book **nǎngsěu phrá'** หนังสือพระ

remember, to **jamdâi** จำได้

remove, to (take off, clothes, shoes) **thòrt** ถอด

rent, to **châu** เช่า

reply/answer **tàwp** ตอบ

request **khǎw** ขอ

reserve, to **jorng** จอง

restaurant **ráan ahǎan** ร้านอาหาร

restroom (bathroom) **hâwng-nám** ห้องน้ำ

retail **bplìik** ปลีก

return, to (go back) **glàp** กลับ; out and back **bpai-glàp** ไปกลับ

rice **khâau** ข้าว; sticky rice **khâau nǐau** ข้าวเหนียว

rice field **naa** นา

rich **ruai** รวย

right (hand) **kwǎa** ขวา

right here/there **dtrong níi** ตรงนี้; **dtrong-nán** ตรงนั้น

river **mâe-náam** แม่น้ำ

road **tha-nǒn** ถนน

roast, roast chicken **gài yâang** ไก่ย่าง

room **hông** ห้อง; single room **hông dîau** ห้องเดี่ยว; double room **hông khûu** ห้องคู่

rubbish **khayà'** ขยะ

run, to **wîng** วิ่ง

run, to run out of something **mòt** หมด; **mâi mii láeu** ไม่มีแล้ว

sad, to be **sǐa-jai** เสียใจ

salary **ngoen-duean** เงินเดือน

sale (reduced prices) **lót-raa-khaa** ลดราคา

salt **gluea** เกลือ

salty (taste) **khem** เค็ม

same, the **mǔean** เหมือน

sandals **rawng-tháo-tàe** รองเท้าแตะ

sauce, dip **nám jîm** น้ำจิ้ม

say, to **bòrk** บอก

scary, frightening **nâa-glua** น่ากลัว

school **rong-rian** โรงเรียน

scolding, (verbal) abuse *kham-dù'dàa* คำดุด่า

sea *thá-le* ทะเล

seafood *aa-hăan-thá-le* อาหารทะเล

search for *hăa* หา

season *rúe-dou* ฤดู

seat *thîi nâng* ที่นั่ง

secondary (school) *matthayom* มัธยม

see *hĕn* เห็น

sell, to *khăai* ขาย

separate, to; to be separated *yâek* แยก

shampoo *chaem-phuu* แชมพู; *yaa sà' phŏm* ยาสระผม

shave *kon* โกน

she *khău* เขา; *lòn* หล่อน

shoe(s) *rorng tháau* รองเท้า

shop *ráan* ร้าน

short (length) *sân* สั้น

short (height) *tîa* เตี้ย

shout *tà-kon* ตะโกน

show *shoh* โชว์; *gaan sa-daeng* การแสดง

shower (or bath) *àap-nám* อาบน้ำ

shrimp/prawn *kûng* กุ้ง

shut, to close *pìt* ปิด

shy *aay, khîi-aay* อาย, ขี้อาย

siblings *phîi-nóng* พี่น้อง

sick, to be sick *bpùai* ป่วย; *mâi sabai* ไม่สบาย

side *khâng* ข้าง

side-street *soi* ซอย

silk cloth *phâa măi* ผ้าไหม

sincere, heartfelt *jing-jai* จริงใจ

sing, to sing (a song) *rórng phlehng* ร้องเพลง

singer *nák rórng* นักร้อง

single, sole *dîau* เดี่ยว; single room *hông dîau* ห้องเดี่ยว; single bed *dtiang dîau* เตียงเดี่ยว

single, unmarried *bpen sòht* เป็นโสด

sister (older) *phîi* พี่; (younger) *nóng* น้อง

sister-in-law (older) *phîi saphái* พี่สะใภ้; (younger) *nóng saphái* น้อง สะใภ้

size *kha-nàat* ขนาด

skilled, good at something *gèng* เก่ง

skin *pyŭ* ผิว

skirt *grà-bprohng* กระโปรง

skytrain *rót fai fáa* รถไฟฟ้า

slander, gossip *nin-thaa* นินทา

sleep, to *làp* หลับ

slowly *cháa-cháa* ช้า ช้า

small *lék* เล็ก

smart *chà-làat* ฉลาด

smelly *mĕn* เหม็น

smile *yím* ยิ้ม

snack, to have a snack *gin lên* กินเล่น

snake *nguu* งู

snooze, to *norn lên* นอนเล่น

soap **sabùu** สบู่

socks **thŭng-tháo** ถุงเท้า

soldier **thá-hăan** ทหาร

sometimes **baang thii** บางที

son **lûuk chaai** ลูกชาย

song **phleng** เพลง

sore/painful **jèp** เจ็บ

sorry (apology) **khăw-thôt** ขอโทษ

sorry (regret) **sĭa-jai** เสียใจ

sound, noise **sĭang** เสียง

south **dtâi** ใต้

speak, to **phûut** พูด

spoon **chórn** ช้อน

sportsman/woman **nák gilaa**
  นัก กิฬา

stairs **bandai** บันได

stand **yuen** ยืน

start/begin **rôem** เริ่ม

state **rát** รัฐ

station **sathăanii** สถานี; railway
  station **sathăanii rót fai** สถานี
  รถไฟ; bus station **sathăanii rót
  bus** สถานีรถบัส

STD **rôhk phûu yǐng** โรคผู้หญิง

steak **sadték** สเต็ก

step- **lîang** เลี้ยง; step child **lûuk
  lîang** ลูกเลี้ยง

sticky rice **khâaw-nǐaw** ข้าวเหนียว

stink **mĕn** เหม็น

stir-fry **phàt** ผัด

stomach-ache **bpùat thórng**
  ปวดท้อง

stop, halt **yùt** หยุด

story, tale, subject, matter **rêuang**
  เรื่อง

stove **tao** เตา

straight on (ahead) **dtrong bpai**
  ตรงไป

stroll, to **deun lên** เดินเล่น

strong **khăeng-raeng** แข็งแรง

student (school) **nák-rian** นักเรียน

student (university) **nák-sùek-săa**
  นักศึกษา

study, to **rian** เรียน

style **bàep** แบบ

sub-district **dtambon (tambon)**
  ตำบล

suffer, to (from illness) **bpen...** เป็น

sugar **nám-dtaan** น้ำตาล

sums, to do (calculate figures) **khít
  lêhk** คิดเลข

supper **ahăan khâm** อาหารค่ำ

sweep (the room) **kwàat-bâan**
  กวาดบ้าน

sweet **wăan** หวาน

sweet/dessert **khăwng-wăan**
  ของหวาน

sweetheart **wăan-jai** หวานใจ;
  khon rák คนรัก

swim **wâay-nám** ว่ายน้ำ

symptom **aagaan** อาการ

table **dtó'** โต๊ะ

tablet, pill **yaa mét** ยาเม็ด

take, to take along, accompany *phaa* พา; pick up *gèp* เก็บ

take, to (time) *gin* กิน

take, to (accept) *au* เอา

talk, to *phûut* พูด

taste (food) *chim* ชิม

tasty (tempting to eat) *nâa-gin* กิน

taxi *rót táeksîi* รถแท็กซี่

tea *chaa* ชา

teach, to *sŏn* สอน

teacher (school) *khruu* ครู; (academic, religious) *ajaan* อาจารย์

teeth, tooth *fan* ฟัน

telephone *thoh-rasàp* โทรศัพท์; *thoh* โทร; to telephone someone *thoh bpai hăa* โทรไปหา; there is a telephone call *thoh maa* โทรมา

tell, to *bòrk* บอก

temple *wát* วัด

ten thousand *mèun* หมื่น

textbook *năngsěu rian* หนังสือ เรียน; *tamraa* ตำรา

than, compared with *gwàa* กว่า

thanks! *khorp-jai!* ขอบใจ (to a younger person)

that (one) *nán* นั้น; (after verbs of saying etc.) *wâa* ว่า

then *láew-kâw* แล้วก็

there *thîi nân* ที่นั่น

they (people only) *khăw* เขา

think, to *khít* คิด; to think over *khít duu* คิดดู

thirsty *hĭu náam* หิวน้ำ

this (one) *nîi* นี้

thoughtfulness, goodwill *nám-jai* น้ำใจ

thousand *phan* พัน

three *săam* สาม

throat *khor* คอ

throw, to (away, out) *thíng* ทิ้ง

ticket *dtŭa* ตั๋ว

tie *nékthai* เน็คไท

time (length of) *wehlaa* เวลา; (occurrence) *khráng* ครั้ง; on time *dtrong wehlaa* ตรงเวลา; all the time *dta-lòrt wehlaa* ตลอดเวลา

timetable *dtaraang wehlaa* ตารางเวลา

tired *nèuai* เหนื่อย

title (name of story) *chêu rêuang* ชื่อเรื่อง

to (going toward) *bpai* ไป

tobacco *yaa sùup* ยาสูบ

today *wan níi* วันนี้

together *gan* กัน

toilet *hông-náam* ห้อง น้ำ

toilet paper *gradàat thít-chûu* กระดาษทิชชู; *gradàat chamrá'* กระดาษชำระ

tomato *má-khŭea-thêt* มะเขือเทศ

tomorrow *phrûng níi* พรุ่งนี้

too (excessively) **gern-bpai** เกินไป

tooth **fan** ฟัน

toothache **bpùat fan** ปวดฟัน

toothbrush **praeng-sǐi-fan** แปรงสีฟัน

toothpaste **yaa sǐi fan** ยาสีฟัน

torch, flashlight **fai-chǎay** ไฟฉาย

touch, to; grasp **jàp** จับ

towel **phâa-chét-tua** ผ้าเช็ดตัว

town **mueang** เมือง

traffic jam **rót dtìt** รถติด

train **rót fai** รถไฟ

translate, to **bplae** แปล

tree **dtôn mái** ต้นไม้

trip, excursion (to go on a trip) **bpai thîau** ไปเที่ยว

trusted, trusted friend **phêuan khûu-jai** เพื่อนคู่ใจ

try, to try out **lorng** ลอง

t-shirt **sêua yêut** เสื้อยืด

turn, to (in another direction) **líaw** เลี้ยว

turn left **líaw-sáay** เลี้ยวซ้าย

turn right **líaw-khwǎa** เลี้ยวขวา

twelve **sìp-sǎwng** สิบสอง

twenty **yîi-sìp** ยี่สิบ

two **sǎng** สอง

ugly **nâa-klìat** น่าเกลียด

umbrella **rôm** ร่ม

uncle **lung** ลุง

uncomfortable **mâi-sà-baay** ไม่สบาย

under (below) **dtâi** ใต้

underground railway **rót fai dtâi din** รถไฟใต้ดิน

understand, to **khâu-jai** เข้าใจ

university **má-hǎa-wít-thá-yaa-lai** มหาวิทยาลัย

unmarried **bpen sòht** เป็นโสด

upper (level) **chán bon** ชั้นบน

upset stomach **thórng sǐa** ท้องเสีย

upstairs **khâng bon** ข้างบน

urgent **dùan** ด่วน

use, to **chái** ใช้

used to **khoei** เคย

usually **pà-kà-tì/pòk-kà-tì** ปกติ

vacant **wâang** ว่าง

vacation/holiday **wan-yùt** วันหยุด

van (vehicle) **rót-tôu** รถตู้

vegetable **phàk** ผัก

vegetarian **mang-sà-wí-rát** มังสวิรัติ

vegetarian (Chinese) **kin-je** กินเจ

venerate, to (worship) **buu-chaa** บูชา

very, very much **mâak** มาก; **yéu'** เยอะ

village **mùu-bâan** หมู่บ้าน

villager **chaau bâan** ชาวบ้าน

visitor (guest) **khàek** แขก

voice/sound **sǐang** เสียง

vomit, to (informal) *ûak* อ้วก;
  (formal) *aajian* อาเจียน

wait a moment (informal)
  raw-dǐew รอเดี๋ยว
wait for *raw* รอ
wake up, to; to get up *dtèun* ตื่น
walk, to *deun* เดิน
want, to want to *yàak* อยาก
warm (weather) *ùn* อุ่น
wash, to (clothes) *sák* ซัก
watch, to; to look at *duu* ดู
water *nám* น้ำ
waterfall *nám-tòk* น้ำตก
way (route; method) *thaang* ทาง;
  way out, exit *thaang òrk* ทางออก
we *rau* เรา
wear *sài* ใส่
weather *aa-kàat* อากาศ
wedding *ngaan-tàeng-ngaan*
  งานแต่งงาน
week *athít* อาทิตย์
well, healthy *sabai dii* สบายดี
what? *arai?* อะไร
when? *mêua-rai?* เมื่อไหร่
where? *thîi nǎi?* ที่ไหน
which? (of several things) *nǎi?* ไหน
white *sǐi khǎau* สีขาว
wholesale *sòng* ส่ง
why *tham-mai* ทำไม
wife (informal) *mia* เมีย; (formal)

phanrayaa ภรรยา; (minor wife,
  mistress) *mia nói* เมียน้อย
wind *lom* ลม
window *nâa-tàng* หน้าต่าง
with *gàp* กับ
with, by *doi* โดย
withdraw (money) *thǎwn-ngoen*
  ถอนเงิน
winter *rúe-dou-nǎaw* ฤดูหนาว
word *kham* คำ
work, to *tham ngaan* ทำงาน
world *lôk* โลก
wound (cut, sore place) *phlǎe* แผล
write, to *khǐan* เขียน
wrong (incorrect) *phìt* ผิด

year *bpii* ปี
yellow *sǐi-lǔeang* สีเหลือง
yes *châi* ใช่
yesterday *mêua waan níi*
  เมื่อวานนี้
you (polite) *khun* คุณ; (intimate)
  ther เธอ; (respectful) *thâan* ท่าน
younger brother *náwng-chaay*
  น้องชาย
younger sister *náwng-sǎaw*
  น้องสาว
your *khǎwng-khun* ของคุณ

zebra *máa-laay* ม้าลาย
zero *sǔun* ศูนย์
zoo *sǔan-sàt* สวนสัตว์

Published by Tuttle Publishing, an imprint of Periplus Editions.

www.tuttlepublishing.com

Copyright © 2007, 2016 by Periplus Editions (HK) Ltd.

All rights reserved.

LCC Card Number: 2006938499
ISBN 978-0-8048-4596-0

Distributed by:

North America, Latin America & Europe
Tuttle Publishing
364 Innovation Drive
North Clarendon, VT 05759-9436, USA
Tel: 1 (802) 773 8930; Fax: 1 (802) 773 6993
info@tuttlepublishing.com
www.tuttlepublishing.com

Japan
Tuttle Publishing
Yaekari Building 3rd Floor
5-4-12 Osaki, Shinagawa-ku
Tokyo 141-0032, Japan
Tel: (81) 3 5437 0171; Fax: (81) 3 5437 0755
sales@tuttle.co.jp; www.tuttle.co.jp

Asia Pacific
Berkeley Books Pte Ltd
61 Tai Seng Avenue #02-12
Singapore 534167
Tel: (65) 6280 1330; Fax: (65) 6280 6290
inquiries@periplus.com.sg
www.periplus.com

19 18 17 16 . 5 4 3 2 1   1603CM

Printed in China

TUTTLE PUBLISHING® is a registered trademark of Tuttle Publishing, a division of Periplus Editions (HK) Ltd.

ABOUT TUTTLE

"Books to Span the East and West"

Our core mission at Tuttle Publishing is to create books which bring people together one page at a time. Tuttle was founded in 1832 in the small New England town of Rutland, Vermont (USA). Our fundamental values remain as strong today as they were then—to publish best-in-class books informing the English-speaking world about the countries and peoples of Asia. The world has become a smaller place today and Asia's economic, cultural and political influence has expanded, yet the need for meaningful dialogue and information about this diverse region has never been greater. Since 1948, Tuttle has been a leader in publishing books on the cultures, arts, cuisines, languages and literatures of Asia. Our authors and photographers have won numerous awards and Tuttle has published thousands of books on subjects ranging from martial arts to paper crafts. We welcome you to explore the wealth of information available on Asia at **www.tuttlepublishing.com**.